"Transformation demands reliability, trust, and measurable business outcomes. *Return on Intelligence* is the playbook executives need. Kristin maps the intersection of AI agents, leadership, and capital performance – a timely guide for any institution ready to drive innovation at scale."

Darrel Hackett, *U.S. CEO, BMO Financial Group*

"This book demystifies the AI revolution and translates it into tangible enterprise outcomes. Kristin's framework bridges the boardroom and the data center, showing leaders how to operationalize return on intelligence at scale."

Claudia Fan Munce, *Board of Directors: Best Buy, BMO Financial Corp, Arteris IP*

"While working to transform our Army, I learned that the Army that maximizes the strengths of both the team and its machines will win the next war. Business is no different. In this book, Kristin gives executives the first playbook I've seen that applies those principles to commercial leadership: how to deploy AI agents with strategic purpose, operational agility, and measurable leadership value."

Lieutenant General Ross Coffman, *Army Futures Command (Retired)*

"As AI moves out of the lab and into the real world, trust and design will matter more than ever. With *Return on Intelligence*, Dr. Milchanowski lays out the playbook for executives, policymakers, and researchers to win by building that trust while simultaneously scaling responsible and competitive AI. We must work together to implement AI now. Only then can we make a transformative and measurable impact."

Glenda Crisp, *President and CEO, Vector Institute*

Return on Intelligence

A call to lead with empathy, this book redefines what transformation means in the age of artificial intelligence. Where most organizations still chase automation and efficiency, Kristin Milchanowski, PhD, reveals a deeper truth: intelligence is not a tool. It is infrastructure. Cutting through the hype and ambiguity that surrounds AI, she bridges the gap between technological deployment and meaningful transformation.

Through 43 governing principles, Milchanowski demonstrates how AI agents can reshape decisions, orchestrate resources, and embed permanence into complex enterprises. She introduces two transformative metrics that quantify how well institutions integrate intelligent systems into their workflows and governance. Drawing from global leadership experience, Milchanowski argues that innovation without empathy is merely efficiency without trust. True intelligence must be earned through ethical design, transparent implementation, and human-centered leadership. With precision and moral clarity, she shows how organizations can move from pilots to permanence, from experiments to ecosystems. The real return, Milchanowski concludes, is measured not in algorithms, but in the trust we build, the empathy we embed, and the promises we keep.

This book is written for senior executives, transformation leaders, policymakers, and technologists who are navigating the frontier of AI adoption, as well as MBA, AI strategy, and leadership students.

Dr. Kristin L. Milchanowski is a force in global AI and quantum leadership and serves as the chief AI and data officer at BMO Financial Group. With a PhD in decision sciences and post-graduate AI studies from the University of Oxford, she now teaches AI as an associate fellow within the Saïd Business School. She has architected AI strategies that fight illicit finance, elevate digital ecosystems, and redefine innovation. Milchanowski previously held roles at EY, Morgan Stanley, and JP Morgan and was formerly an advisory board member of Automobili Lamborghini.

Return on Intelligence

A Strategic Enterprise Playbook for Scalable AI Agents

Kristin L. Milchanowski, PhD

Routledge
Taylor & Francis Group
NEW YORK AND LONDON

Designed cover image: Getty Images© Credit: cundra.

First published 2026
by Routledge
605 Third Avenue, New York, NY 10158

and by Routledge
4 Park Square, Milton Park, Abingdon, Oxon, OX14 4RN

Routledge is an imprint of the Taylor & Francis Group, an informa business

ISBN: 978-1-041-26299-2 (hbk)
ISBN: 978-1-041-26298-5 (pbk)
ISBN: 978-1-003-74989-9 (ebk)

DOI: 10.4324/9781003749899

Typeset in Times New Roman
by Apex CoVantage, LLC

To Sebastian – a reminder that intelligence, when built with empathy, fulfills the deepest promise of progress: to serve humanity, not replace it. May you always lead with both heart and precision.

Contents

Figures and Tables

Foreword

Artificial intelligence has arrived at the intersection of promise and peril. It offers to create new revenue streams, unlock unprecedented efficiencies, and fundamentally reshape how we work, learn, and create value. Yet for all its transformative potential, AI's greatest challenge lies not in the technology itself, but in our human and institutional capacity to absorb rapid change while maintaining human trust. Kristin's book provides what leadership teams urgently need: a practical game plan – 43 principles drawn from actual implementation – for navigating this transformation responsibly. Every boardroom from London to New York now grapples with the same question: how to embrace transformative technology while evolving culture. Kristin understands that this is more than a technology challenge. After three decades of implementing change in large organizations, I recognize that success requires something more nuanced than disruption – it demands what I call "prudent innovation." The speed of change distinguishes our current moment. The industrial revolution unfolded over generations, and computerization evolved across decades, but artificial intelligence compresses transformation into quarters and years. Organizations face the paradox of moving at startup speed while maintaining the trust and stability that institutions provide. This tension sits at the heart of modern leadership.

Consider how my own organization, BMO Financial Group, is navigating these waters. We are hiring technologists to build AI systems while investing heavily in workforce development. We are redesigning the bank to combine human judgment with machine intelligence. These efforts come from an understanding that competitive advantage emerges not from AI alone, but from the integration of human creativity and machine capability. It is culture and leadership that will shape the effectiveness of execution.

The great contribution captured within *Return on Intelligence* lies in recognizing that leadership in the AI era is about managing tensions. Leaders must automate tasks without dehumanizing work. They must eliminate routine functions while building new skills. They must generate excitement while addressing legitimate fears about the future of work. Kristin's principles navigate these challenges with hard-won wisdom. Consider the first principle: "Business Before Buzz," arguing that AI should never be introduced as a shiny new toy. Instead, it must be tied to a core business goal. Within is an example of a global insurer whose chatbot failed to gain traction as an "innovation" but saw its adoption triple once it was repositioned as a tool to recover revenue – turning a tech curiosity into an essential asset. It is this kind of practical insight that makes the book so valuable.

This explains why Kristin's emphasis on cross-functional leadership resonates so powerfully. The command-and-control structures of the industrial age cannot orchestrate transformation at this scale. Success requires harmonizing varied voices – from finance professionals to AI scientists to human resources leaders – into coherent action. Leadership becomes less about commanding and more about conducting. The human dimension demands particular attention. Workforce anxieties about AI run deep, echoing historical patterns of technological disruption. Yet history also shows that while technology displaces certain jobs, it ultimately creates new categories of human contribution. The challenge for leaders today is to be honest about impending changes while articulating a credible vision for humans flourishing alongside artificial intelligence. In a corporate environment, this is the evolution of mindset from job tasks to careers. The book's tactical focus on specific leadership roles provides essential guidance. The CEO must articulate a vision while managing stakeholder anxieties. The CFO must quantify AI investments while accepting uncertainty. The CHRO must reimagine workforce development while maintaining engagement. Yet beyond these tactical concerns lies a deeper challenge: maintaining an organization's purpose amid radical change.

The 2008 financial crisis offered a stark lesson in what happens when innovation outpaces governance. The institutions that emerged strongest understood that sustainable innovation requires resilience. This concept extends beyond risk management to encompass an organization's capacity to learn and relearn while preserving its core values. Three pillars support this resilience. First, ensuring AI skills and tools extend throughout the organization rather than remain confined to specialists. Second, building ethical frameworks before crises emerge, not after. And third, making sure that technology serves human needs rather than displaces them. The profound irony of artificial intelligence is that as machines become more capable, distinctly human qualities – judgment, creativity, wisdom, empathy – become more valuable. The greatest risk we face is not technological unemployment but human disengagement from the work itself. When workers see no path to meaningful contribution, organizations risk losing not just talent but their purpose.

Return on Intelligence equips leaders with practical tools for avoiding that fate. The 43 principles offer a framework for continuous adaptation, acknowledging that transformation requires not just new technologies but also new mindsets, not just process change but also cultural evolution. The question is not whether artificial intelligence will transform our organizations – that has already begun. The question is whether we will shape it consciously, ethically, and in service of human flourishing. The real return on intelligence, artificial or otherwise, lies not in cost reductions but in our enhanced capacity to solve complex problems and create meaningful work. Kristin's book helps leadership teams achieve that return, transforming AI from a source of deep-seated anxiety into an engine of institutional renewal and human progress.

By Mona E. Malone

Preface

Return on intelligence is the measurable value created when insight, not just automation, becomes a capital asset that compounds enterprise value over time.

When I began writing *Return on Intelligence*, the conversation around AI was dominated by headlines and hype. Every enterprise wanted transformation, but few could define what transformation actually meant, and hardly anyone knew what was needed to implement and scale. Most programs were still chasing proof of concepts while executives were already under pressure to show proof of value. This book was born from that tension. Over the past decade, I have watched too many organizations deploy technology faster than they deploy trust. They confuse automation with intelligence, and activity with impact. *Return on Intelligence* exists to correct that imbalance.

In the course of leading teams across industries and continents, I learned something enduring: "Innovation without empathy is merely efficiency without trust." I did not learn that from a conference stage or a research paper. I learned it in the quiet moments after major deployments, when success metrics were met but something essential was missing. It was the hesitation in a manager's voice before adopting a new tool, the unease of a client who felt analyzed but not understood, the fatigue of teams asked to adapt without being heard. Empathy, I discovered, is more than a virtue; it is a structural advantage. It is the invisible architecture that determines whether intelligence earns permission to operate. When empathy is embedded, technology amplifies human potential. When it is absent, even the most advanced systems erode belief.

These pages are a playbook for leadership and offer a framework for turning AI agents into a measurable advantage – ethically, transparently, and with human trust engineered into every layer. I wrote this book because the future of hybrid intelligence will not be defined by how great our AI models are, but by how wisely we build with them.

The true return on intelligence is measured in the trust we build, the empathy we embed, and the promises we keep.

Innovation without empathy is merely efficiency without trust.

Acknowledgments

Above all, for a promise – that progress can be both powerful and principled.

I owe gratitude to Darryl White, Darrel Hackett, Mona Malone, Steve Tennyson, and my BMO Financial Group colleagues who champion the vision of scalable, human-centered intelligence. To Dontá Wilson, thank you for being both counsel and mirror, you reflect proof that the most powerful equations are written not in code or capital, but in trust, loyalty, and the rare symmetry of minds. My deep appreciation extends to Dr. Ashish Vaswani, Ken Durazzo, and LTG Ross Coffman, whose friendship sharpens me and whose insight continues to shape the architecture of our shared future. To the U.S. Army Futures Command, Special Competitive Studies Project, Vector Institute, and Perimeter Institute for pushing the frontiers of Applied Intelligence. To my academic collaborators for their intellectual partnership at Oxford University Saïd Business School: Dr. Andrew Stephen, Dr. Felipe Thomaz, Dr. Gregory Clark, Dr. Alex Connock, and DipAI'21. And Democritus University of Thrace: Dr. Ioannis Karafyllidis and Dr. Panagiotis Dimitrakis. Thank you, Isabel Schaad, Dr. Richard Padbury, and Carl Roberts, for bringing structure and precision to this project and my life. To my parents, for unwavering faith in me. To Meredith Norwich and the Routledge editorial team for the opportunity.

Key Terms

AI Agents – Goal-oriented, autonomous systems created by humans that perceive, decide, and act within a constrained environment defined by their human designers. Unlike traditional software, their outcomes are not pre-coded.

AI Orchestration – Coordinating and managing multiple AI agents to work together across workflows.

Agent Leverage Multiplier – The productivity elasticity created by AI augmentation.

Agent Stack – The technical layers (models, logic, interfaces) that make up an AI agent's architecture.

Hybrid Intelligence – Collaboration between humans and machines for better outcomes.

Human-to-Agent Ratio (Human:Agent Ratio) – A measure of competitiveness showing the balance of human talent to AI agents capacity in an organization.

Intelligent Operating Leverage (IOL) – Measures the incremental output or operating efficiency achieved per unit change in the Human:Agent mix, modified from the classical financial measure of Operating Leverage.

Intelligent Operating Leverage Model – Includes six drivers of enterprise value: Revenue Expansion, Cost Efficiency, Risk Optimization, Experience Differentiation, Trust & Transparency, and Intelligent Operating Leverage.

Operating Leverage (OL) – Traditional measures of how a change in revenue translates into a change in operating income (EBIT).

Return on Intelligence (ROI_2) – The measurable value an agent creates when insight itself becomes an accretive asset.

Return on Investment (ROI) – Traditional measure of financial gain or loss from an investment.

Introduction

Scaling Smart in an Era of Hybrid Intelligence With AI Agents

Every corporate era is defined by what it optimizes for. The industrial age optimized for scale. The digital age optimized for speed. This next era of **hybrid intelligence**, the collaboration between humans and machines, will be defined by what enterprises optimize for next: return on intelligence. **Return on intelligence (ROI_2)** is the measurable value an agent creates when insight itself becomes an accretive asset. The playbooks of efficiency, digitization, and automation are no longer enough to compete. Markets now demand systems that are faster, more adaptive, and more intelligent – systems that not only execute but also decide, learn, and continually reshape the institutions they serve. That shift is embodied in the rise of **artificial intelligence agents**. Agents represent more than just technology; they signify a new class of worker, one that operates at speeds and scales beyond human capacity but still demands governance, accountability, and integration akin to any senior appointment. As agents gain the ability to serve ten thousand customers in real time, simulate market scenarios before they unfold, and fully audit every transaction rather than just sampling, they are redefining roles, transforming leadership dynamics, and shifting organizational politics.

Within lies a blueprint for leaders to seize advantage through ***Return on Intelligence: A Strategic Enterprise Playbook for Scalable AI Agents,*** equipping organizations to win by turning adoption into legitimacy, legitimacy into momentum, and momentum into enduring market power. This book is written for those determined to lead the AI era. Written for leaders, CEOs, CFOs, CIOs, CHROs, CMOs, and the next generation of transformation executives who are tasked with answering the board's most challenging questions:

- *How do we separate hype from fundamental value?*
- *What metrics prove that this is working?*
- *How do we balance human capital with digital capacity?*
- *Who owns the outcomes of agent deployment?*

DOI: 10.4324/9781003749899-1

- *What story will we tell to investors, regulators, and employees about this transformation?*

If you are responsible for strategy, transformation, technology, finance, talent, or marketing, this book gives you the playbook to scale AI agents. Future success hinges on scaling these agents wisely. You do not need another AI strategy deck. You need a set of moves. Because the truth is, AI does not win on merit. It wins on momentum. These are the principles that create that momentum.

The question is no longer whether artificial intelligence will reshape industries, but how quickly an enterprise can scale and who within the organization will control the influence it creates. Organizations that fail to move from experimentation to scaled execution won't just fall behind; they will lose their relevance. At the heart of this transformation is the rise of AI agents: digital workers designed not just to automate isolated tasks, but also to function as part of institutional teams. These agents do more than work; they fundamentally change how work is accomplished. Operating at the intersection of data, decision-making, and delivery, they can execute entire workflows and adapt in real time as circumstances change. When properly designed, deployed, and governed, agents become the connective tissue of the modern enterprise. AI agents are goal-oriented, autonomous systems created by humans that perceive, decide, and act within a constrained environment defined by their human designers. Unlike traditional software, their outcomes are not pre-coded. This book is about building that connective tissue intelligently, strategically, and credibly.

From Automation to Agency

Many organizations mistakenly view agents as the next step in automation. However, they are fundamentally different. Traditional automation relies on scripts that are repeatable, predictable, and strictly defined. In contrast, agents are adaptive, contextual, and capable of making decisions within established guardrails. This marks a shift from mere process efficiency to enterprise intelligence. But intelligence at scale is not a technology problem; it is a leadership problem. Enterprises do not fail at transformation because the algorithms fail. They fail because leaders underestimate the politics of adoption, the necessity of measurement, and the need to tie technology back to outcomes that matter to shareholders, regulators, and customers. Scaling agents is not a story of technology. It is a story of **influence**, who gains it, who loses it, and who knows how to wield it.

Why This Matters Now

Markets are unforgiving. Cost pressures are intensifying. Compliance complexity grows with every regulation. Digital-first competitors are redefining customer expectations daily. Against this backdrop, the companies that scale agents first and do so with discipline gain not just efficiency but also influence. Consider the Human:Agent ratio. Just as past generations measured productivity in revenue per employee, the next generation will measure competitiveness by the balance of human talent and agent capacity. Organizations that govern this ratio proactively set targets, embed them in scorecards, and link them to return on investment (ROI) will turn adoption into an advantage. Those who ignore it will drift into irrelevance, consumed by fragmented pilots and rising skepticism. The clock is ticking. Competitors are not waiting for perfect clarity. They are experimenting, scaling, and compressing the time window in which your enterprise can lead. Once parity is reached, differentiation will require exponentially greater investment. To lead in this new era, enterprises must go beyond adoption and build intelligence into the very fabric of their organizations.

What This Book Offers

Return on Intelligence: A Strategic Enterprise Playbook for Scalable AI Agents is not a technical manual. It is not a catalog of use cases. It is a strategic guide, 43 principles, for executives who must turn AI agents from curiosity into competitive advantage. This book unfolds in three deliberate parts: Foundation, Influence, and Governance. Together, they form a maturity arc: define intelligently, lead persuasively, and govern credibly. Each part of this book builds upon the last, but you can enter at the stage that matches your organization's maturity:

- If you're still clarifying strategy, begin with Part I – Foundation.
- If you're navigating sponsorship, start with Part II – Influence.
- If you're designing governance frameworks, go directly to Part III – Governance.
- If you're short on time, go directly to Principle 20 and Chapters 8 and 9.

Part I – Foundation: Strategy, Design, and Economic Legitimacy

The first movement builds the scaffolding for intelligent enterprises. We begin with clarity: what agents are, why they matter now, and how they differ from traditional automation. We then explore design principles that marry human trust with engineering discipline, and we close by proving the economic case. This part moves the reader from curiosity to conviction – from innovation theater to investable infrastructure. Inside, you will find:

- **Chapter 1: Strategic Deployment and Execution:** Why AI agents matter now, and how they differ from traditional automation.
- **Chapter 2: Design Principles and Engineering Discipline:** How to build agents that people want to use and trust.
- **Chapter 3: Economic Justification and Return on Investment:** How to justify agents with ROI metrics that satisfy the CFO, investors, and regulators.

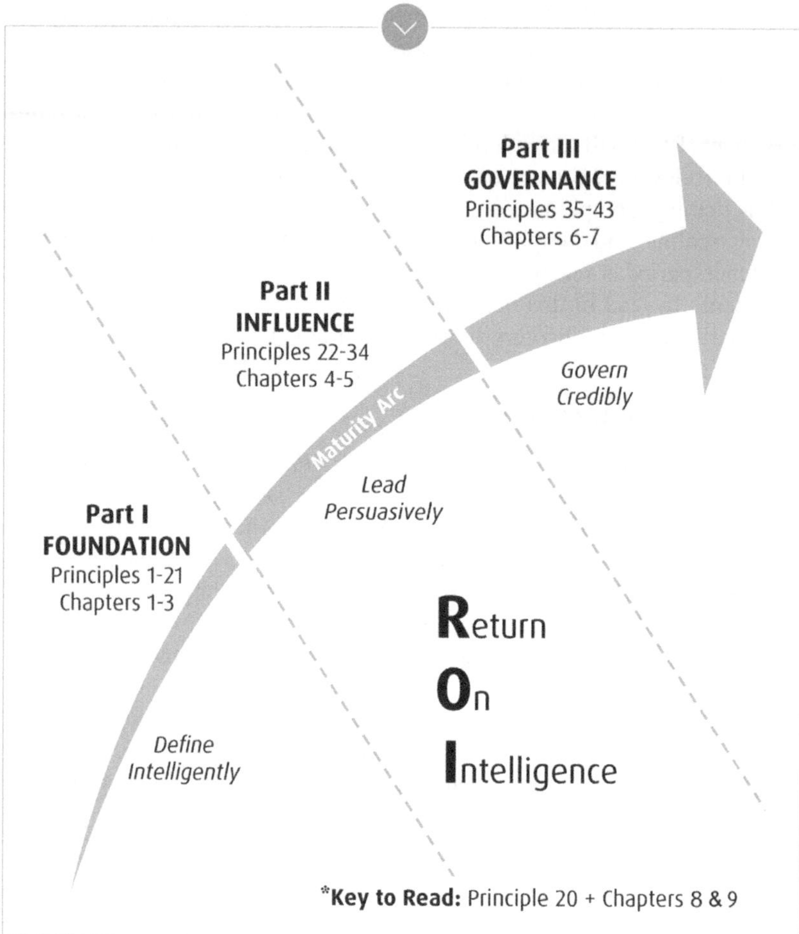

Figure I.1 Return on Intelligence maturity arc. Diagram by Kristin Milchanowski and Isabel Schaad.

Part II – Influence: Leadership, Culture, and Organizational Transformation

The second movement confronts a hard truth: adoption is political. Technology alone does not transform an organization; leadership choreography does. This section explores how to stage visible wins, align power centers, and manage cultural readiness. It introduces the subtle art of narrative sequencing – the psychology behind why one success story travels faster than ten reports. It also defines adaptability as a strategic muscle: the capacity for continuous learning, not episodic reform. Inside, you will find:

- **Chapter 4: Leadership, Influence, and Political Buy-In:** How to stage wins, manage narratives, and secure buy-in across the C-suite and frontline.
- **Chapter 5: Innovation, Ecosystem, and Adaptability:** How to embed agents into the organizational DNA, shifting from project to doctrine.

Part III – Governance: Trust, Transparency, and Scalable Momentum

The final movement turns success into a system. It codifies how enterprises earn and sustain trust through governance, selective transparency, and measurable performance. Here, the conversation shifts from adoption to accountability. How do you build dashboards that signal reliability to regulators and investors alike? How do you scale without losing control? Governance becomes not a brake on progress, but the architecture that allows it to accelerate safely. Inside, you will find:

- **Chapter 6: Trust, Transparency, and Selectivity:** How to track adoption, govern ratios, and turn outcomes into credibility.
- **Chapter 7: Adoption, Scale, and User-Centricity:** How to earn enterprise trust.

Across these three parts, *Return on Intelligence* offers a playbook for executives who must balance speed with stewardship and who understand that power without principles is fragility disguised as innovation. Each chapter introduces a set of **principles** and strategic maxims for designing, deploying, and scaling agents. They are blunt, practical, and unambiguous. Some will challenge conventional wisdom, and others will expose the hidden traps that sink well-intentioned transformations. All principles are designed to give executives both the language and the levers to lead. To show how the chapters' principles are understood across leadership roles, five personas are presented: Chief Strategy & Transformation Officer, Chief Financial Officer, Chief Technology Officer, Chief Human Resources Officer, and Chief Marketing Officer. These personas are fictional but are based on real-world experience, helping readers see what is most important to each stakeholder type and how agent deployment is perceived across the C-suite.

The AI-Native CEO: Designing for Intelligence Across the 4Rs

In the intelligence-driven economy, relevance must be treated as a dynamic capability. For senior executives and enterprise leaders, becoming native to artificial intelligence is not about technical skill. It is about designing organizations where intelligence is embedded with intention, scale, and empathy. Advantage now depends on deep integration across capital allocation, workforce design, product development, and enterprise risk. The future will be led by those who treat artificial intelligence as a platform for reinvention, one that understands and responds with human-centered empathy. Those who move with clarity will compound intelligence. Those who wait will follow.

This transformation is already underway, and its impact can be understood through four strategic dimensions:

1. **Risk:** Enabling real-time fraud detection, dynamic credit decisioning, and adaptive surveillance.
2. **Revenue:** Unlocking margin through hyper-personalized offers, precision cross-sell, and dynamic pricing.
3. **Resilience:** Automating complex workflows to reduce cost and error while ensuring continuity.
4. **Relationships:** Serving clients as segments of one through intelligent, contextual engagement.

AI agents are no longer optional; they are foundational. The era of intelligent enterprise design has begun. Leaders who act with urgency and scale AI agents with empathy will define the future. This book is your guide. The blueprint is here. The moment is now.

Part I

Foundation

Strategy, Design, and Economic Legitimacy

Within Part I, strategic foundations are established that distinguish intelligent deployment from digital enthusiasm. Agents are strategic assets and require clear business linkage, precise design, and measurable economic justification. Leaders who approach AI as a sandbox will generate novelty; those who approach it as infrastructure will generate returns. Part I reframes the "why" behind agents (Chapter 1), defines the design principles that make them both craveable and credible (Chapter 2), and grounds it all in economic rigor (Chapter 3). Together, these form the architecture of legitimacy: strategy before theater, trust before launch, and numbers before narrative. When executed with discipline, agents stop being experiments and start being investments.

DOI: 10.4324/9781003749899-2

Chapter 1

Strategic Deployment and Execution

Strategic execution is the difference between ideas that linger and ideas that lead. In AI, the enemy is not bad technology; it is mistimed rollouts, misaligned motives, and mismanaged scale. This chapter reframes agent deployment not as an IT initiative, but as a sequence of power moves. Each principle in this section gives executives tools to build momentum, reduce resistance, and execute with political foresight. Strategic execution is not a technical challenge; it is a leadership imperative. In many global organizations, executive teams sit atop a backlog of AI pilots and prototypes that never achieved scale. The issue is rarely competence, but rather alignment. Ideas get lost between departments, roadmaps, and review boards. Executives make the fatal error of deploying agents like apps: fast, broad, and without a disciplined strategy. What gets overlooked is that each AI deployment sends a political signal. If done poorly, it triggers antibodies in the culture, posing a threat to legacy systems, teams, and incentives. Done well, it becomes an accelerant of influence, credibility, and measurable value. Agent deployment should not be treated like a systems upgrade. Instead, it is a deliberate choreography of influence. Each principle within is designed to give decision-makers strategic range: the ability to pace, prioritize, and position their agent strategy in a way that feels natural to stakeholders and unignorable to rivals. These principles come from some of the world's most formidable transformations, where influence was not just maintained during digital change, but was also multiplied. Real strategy is not about being fast; it is about being first in the minds of those who matter. And that starts with moving in rhythm with your organization's appetite, not within your innovation agenda.

Principle 1: Business Before Buzz

Definition: Tie agent deployment to business outcomes, not innovation agendas.

AI agents are not toys and should not be introduced merely as experiments if the goal is actual adoption, budget approval, and credibility. Principle 1 directs

DOI: 10.4324/9781003749899-3

leaders to approach AI not as a novelty, but as a tool with measurable business value. This principle changes the narrative, moving AI out of speculation and into practical business performance and relevance. When executives align AI agent deployment with the company's strategic priorities, perceptions shift from viewing AI as a shiny new object to recognizing it as a strategic asset. They move from seeking approval to leading with proven results. If agents are introduced only as part of a tech-forward "innovation agenda," they risk being sidelined, tested, and critiqued without urgency. In contrast, when linked to key performance indicators (KPIs) that drive growth, margin, or risk reduction, AI secures a place at the decision-making table. Behavioral psychology shows people are more motivated by loss aversion than by potential gain. If AI agents are positioned as tools to prevent margin leakage, resolve frontline bottlenecks, or unlock trapped revenue in operations, they become essential. Buzz fades; business drives action.

Why It Matters to Corporations: When AI agents are introduced as "innovation," they are treated like toys. When tied to business KPIs, they become essential. This principle ensures that AI is not seen as a technical pet project, but a profit and loss (P&L) driven strategic move. Innovation does not sell in the boardroom; impact does. To maximize impact, AI agents must be tied directly to key outcomes such as improving margins, growing revenue, reducing risks, or accelerating speed. Hype and buzzwords won't scale; only business results matter. Too often, AI initiatives start in innovation labs and suffer from "sandbox syndrome": promising ideas that never reach real business use. Companies aren't interested in how futuristic a technology seems; they care about measurable impact. This principle stands against the tendency to prioritize novelty over value in corporate strategy. Leaders should demand a clear ROI, not just excitement over AI. Like any capital investment, agents must be evaluated for return, alignment with business metrics, and adoption potential. Viewed as a cost, AI is expendable; tied to key metrics, it becomes indispensable. Consider how often AI agents are showcased in internal demos or conference decks as proof of innovation. And yet those same agents remain unused six months later. Why? Because no one tied their existence to a business need. A well-known pharmaceutical company had a series of AI tools to help with internal onboarding. It wasn't until the same tools were retooled to shorten compliance approval cycles, which impacted time-to-market by 19%, that the CFO signed off on a company-wide deployment. Innovation may open the door, but business value keeps it from closing.

Real-World Example: At a global insurer, the AI team's chatbot failed to gain traction until it was repositioned as a revenue-recovery agent in collections. Once reframed, adoption tripled, and the CFO became the program sponsor. This case study is not an outlier; it is a blueprint: the same bot, the same technology, the same team, but radically different framing. Before the pivot, the agent was filed under "digital innovation," and no executive owned it. Post-pivot, it sat under collections, had a performance dashboard, and was directly tied to quarterly goals. The only change was alignment to business value; it was not a change in tech. What executives must take away from this is simple: AI agents are not neutral. Their perceived legitimacy depends entirely on who sponsors them and the problem they are associated with. No agent should be deployed without a business owner who has a metric at stake. CFOs, COOs, and heads of operations are not just stakeholders; they are drivers of change. Frame the agent as an innovation, and you'll spark curiosity. Frame it as a revenue enabler, and you'll attract capital.

Principle 2: Outcomes Matter

Definition: Design for business outcomes.

Every agent initiative should start with clear, measurable objectives and specific key results that will signal success. Without a defined objective and key results (OKR) framework, even the most advanced AI agent can lack direction, much like a sophisticated ship without a compass and drifting aimlessly. This principle mandates that before code is written, application programming interfaces (APIs) are connected, or models are fine-tuned, leadership must articulate precisely what the agent is intended to accomplish, and how its performance will be measured in ways that matter to the business. OKRs give agents purpose beyond novelty. They translate abstract ambitions, like "improve customer service" or "optimize operations," into specific, measurable outcomes: for example, reducing average customer service handling time by 25% in six months, increasing first-contact resolution to 85%, or cutting the cost-to-serve by $2 million a year. By linking agent design to OKRs from inception, you prevent the trap of building "technology in search of a problem." You give the deployment team a shared definition of success, align cross-functional expectations, and ensure leadership can see the direct link between the agent's work and enterprise value. This precision builds credibility for future AI investments and keeps teams focused.

Why It Matters to Corporations: In large organizations, AI agents risk becoming proof-of-concept experiments that win applause in pilot phases but never make it into production at scale. The reason? Lack of a concrete, shared definition of success that ties back to strategic priorities. OKRs provide the missing link. They turn vague goals into measurable results, ensuring that stakeholders, whether technical, operational, or executive, are aligned on what "good" looks like. Companies that incorporate OKRs into the agent lifecycle see three key benefits:

1. **Strategic Alignment Across the Enterprise:** Every AI investment should ladder directly into the company's strategic objectives, whether that is market share growth, operational efficiency, customer satisfaction, or regulatory

compliance. An OKR-driven agent roadmap makes this link visible to the board and C-suite.

2. **Budget and Political Capital Protection:** OKRs create a performance contract for the agent. When progress is measurable, leaders can defend funding and expansion because they can point to tangible, agreed-upon outcomes.
3. **Operational Focus and Accountability:** In complex organizations, AI teams can be pulled in multiple directions by stakeholders with conflicting needs. OKRs act as guardrails, ensuring prioritization decisions focus on business-critical results rather than opportunistic requests.

Without this discipline, even well-designed agents risk delivering fragmented value, making them harder to justify during budget cycles and more vulnerable to political shifts.

Real-World Example: At a global retail bank, the AI strategy team was assigned to develop an "intelligent onboarding agent" to streamline account openings. While initial enthusiasm was high, after six months, stakeholders questioned the ROI. The team kept adding features without a shared success metric. Midway, the CIO introduced an OKR framework, setting the goal to reduce the average account opening time from 14 days to 3 days within a year. Key results included:

- Achieve 90% accuracy in automated document verification.
- Reduce manual processing time by 60%.
- Maintain compliance audit pass rates at 99%.

With this clarity, the AI development team focused on features that directly impacted key metrics. Within nine months, the agent achieved all three key results: reducing operational costs by $4.5 million annually and decreasing customer churn during onboarding by 20%. When the CFO shared these outcomes with the board, the business case for expanding the agent to additional product lines was clear. An AI agent's longevity and impact depend not on novelty or technical complexity, but on alignment with measurable business value. The OKR framework shifts agent deployment from a trial to a focused, strategic investment. By planning with the end goal in mind, you create a shared definition of success from day one, prevent scope drift and resource dilution, and build the political and financial capital needed to sustain momentum.

In an environment where corporate AI budgets are scrutinized and executive patience is limited, clarity is a competitive advantage. OKRs do not just guide development, they also protect the initiative, validate the investment, and accelerate adoption. Adopt this principle rigorously and make this the first question every AI agent proposal must answer: *What is the objective, and how will we measure it?* If you cannot answer that, you are not ready to build.

Principle 3: Code to the Conclusion

Definition: Define the end state before you code the first prompt.

This principle insists on a reversal of how most organizations approach AI development. Rather than asking what the model can do, the strategic leader asks, *What must this agent prove?* Code to the outcome, not the capability. Define the business value, adoption threshold, stakeholder sponsor, and measurable success metrics before coding any agent. Adopting an outcome-first engineering approach generates clear targets, making the agent and its code accountable for a clear, disciplined ROI feature. This principle empowers leaders to direct AI teams with precision. It reframes AI from open-ended exploration to execution with a purpose.

Why It Matters to Corporations: Most failed AI projects do not fail because the technology did not work. AI projects fail because no one defined what success looked like before building. "We'll see what the model finds" is a liability, not a strategy. Enterprises operate under capital constraints, political scrutiny, and opportunity costs. That is why this principle matters. Corporations need precision alignment between what they build and what they need. When AI agents are scoped without a clearly defined end state, such as "Let's see what this model can uncover in client data," teams tend to build generic solutions in hopes of finding relevance, which leads to struggles with adoption. But when the objective is defined from the start, such as, "This agent should reduce client onboarding time by 40% while surfacing compliance gaps," then every design choice, prompt structure, and user interface (UI) decision serves that goal. In a corporation's power structure, clear goals protect the AI team. It shifts the narrative from "Why did this fail?" to "Did we meet the goal?" It enables objective reviews, faster iteration, and sponsor confidence. In a world where budgets are always contested, clarity is armor.

This principle also reduces waste. In behavioral psychology, we know that "goal dilution" happens when too many outcomes are sought at once. Projects that try to be all things to all stakeholders often fail to satisfy any. Coding to the conclusion creates coherence. When you can tell stakeholders, "Here's what this agent will do, here's how we'll know, and here's the signal of success," you have a trust-building mechanism, and you communicate competence. Clarity creates confidence. People are more engaged when they know what success looks like and how they contribute. Defining the end state enhances team motivation, sponsor clarity, and rollout confidence. So write the success story and explain the finish line before the first prompt is written, and code with a conclusion in mind. Because the most potent agents are not necessarily the ones with the best features, they are the ones that accomplish what they were created to do.

Real-World Example: A regional health system created a generative AI agent to help with clinical documentation. The team was skilled, and the model was state-of-the-art. However, there was no clear final goal. Success metrics were vague: "Make note-taking easier." Without specific objectives, features expanded uncontrollably. The agent became complex, usage dropped, and trust eroded. The turnaround came from the CIO, who redefined the scope. The agent's new goal: reduce documentation time by 25% while improving note completeness as measured by audit scores. That clarity refocused development. Prompts were trimmed, the UI simplified, and training tied to those two KPIs. Within two months of relaunch, note time fell 31%, audit scores rose, and usage stabilized at 89% across departments. The agent did not change fundamentally, but the clarity of its end state transformed its performance. The lesson? Vague ambition sabotages success.

Clear outcomes discipline the build. When you code to a conclusion, every decision becomes accountable. Accountable agents deliver results. Start with the win and then work backward. That is the essence of Principle 3. It sounds obvious, but it is rarely practiced. Most AI programs start with exploration. Curiosity is encouraged. In corporate settings, clarity ensures budget allocation, team alignment, and efficient time use. Establishing success criteria, such as better, smarter, faster, cheaper, or safer, anchors every design, prompt, and performance review to these standards. This process isn't about restricting creativity, but rather purposefully guiding it. Clearly defined success criteria create a framework that fosters innovation. When the end goal is clear, engineering becomes precise. When the goal is fixed, the scope becomes defendable. It encourages healthier relationships among tech, business, and executive stakeholders.

Principle 4: Launch in Silence

Definition: Shift silently; avoid announcing the agent strategy before execution.

A bit of discretion is advised until the first successful delivery happens. If revealed too early, the program might attract attention, generate discussion, and face internal opposition. Early announcements make AI seem merely hypothetical. First, delivering a product makes it real. Authority is built on outcomes, not on intention. People judge new initiatives not on potential, but on early proof. Premature communication increases psychological reactance. Psychological reactance is the impulse to resist what feels imposed. Keeping agent deployment under wraps until proof points exist circumvents organizational antibodies. You are not hiding; you are staging. Silence is not secrecy. It is a strategy.

Why It Matters to Corporations: Corporations are social systems filled with stakeholders, influencers, skeptics, and political actors. In this environment, ideas are not judged solely on their merit; they are evaluated by timing, who presents them, and how well they align with perceived agendas. When a company loudly announces its AI agenda before achieving any success, it introduces risk without adding value. Questions arise: Who owns it? What budget was spent? What jobs will it affect? These are valid questions, but until there are measurable wins, they tend to lead to delays, defensiveness, or even sabotage. Launching in silence allows the team to test, iterate, and secure outcomes before internal resistance forms. Silence protects momentum. A Fortune 200 logistics company launched its first AI agent quietly in its returns processing unit. No fanfare, no cross-departmental steering committee. Within two months, processing time dropped by 48%, errors declined by 22%, and $1.3M in recoveries were achieved. Only then did the COO begin to socialize the program. When performance speaks first, politics listens second. This principle counters the corporate reflex to advertise transformation before it is earned. Silence grants optionality under Principle 4 and minimizes uncertainty by replacing speculation with proof. It gives space to assess performance, evolve the model, or even shut it down without reputational damage. If you need early adopters, recruit them privately. Stage organizational buy-in, and let your first results be the first headline. Silence is not weakness. It is signal control. In the early stages of agent deployment, attention is dangerous. Noise attracts critics. Data attracts supporters. The most seasoned executives know that political capital is earned through controlled outcomes, not early announcements.

Real-World Example: A major North American technology and media company, known for its streaming and cloud-delivery platforms, developed an AI agent to optimize real-time power allocation at its U.S. data centers. Instead of making a public or internal announcement, the head of infrastructure chose a quiet, controlled rollout at just one facility. The tool was described as an operational-efficiency module, seamlessly added to existing monitoring dashboards, rather than as an "AI transformation." For six weeks, engineers used it without knowing that AI was driving it. During this pilot, the facility achieved a 9% reduction in peak power consumption and an 18% stabilization in temperature variance, lowering cooling costs. After verifying these improvements, the executive sponsor sent a memo: "New optimization system has improved efficiency and grid resilience; expansion to the next four sites begins next quarter."

The quiet rollout sparked curiosity, not resistance, and the team sidestepped the politics of "AI panic." No one felt blindsided, so no one mobilized against it. This approach worked by harnessing the power of perception: when people uncover value organically, they advocate for it; when imposed from above, they resist. Launching quietly not only protected the agent but also preserved leadership credibility. Here, silence wasn't about hiding but about building momentum before skeptics could intervene. A strong agent strategy unfolds like a campaign: early wins become internal case studies, and advocates arise not from persuasion but from results. Silence allows the agent to grow in both capability and credibility. There is a secondary benefit: internal team morale. When agents are deployed quietly and start performing, the implementing teams feel ownership and pride. Their input matters. Their concerns are addressed directly. They are not being shown a glossy vision; they are building it. That internal ownership becomes an asset as the program scales. Behaviorally, silence leverages the "IKEA effect," in which people place greater value on things they've helped create. Launching early agents quietly allows for co-creation, iteration, and emotional investment. When the program scales, it already has internal advocates. Ultimately, Principle 4 is about strategic restraint. Speak once you have achieved success. Promote your accomplishments after delivering results. Let the agent take the spotlight. In enterprise transformation, influence is based on results, not words.

Principle 5: Deploy Decisively

Definition: Deploy agents with purpose, not hesitation.

In the realm of enterprise transformation politics, hesitation is a flaw. Principle 5 advises leaders to commit to agent deployment with clarity, conviction, and control. Half-hearted efforts damage credibility. Uncertainty breeds resistance. The most effective implementations are those that move with intention. Not just with speed, but purpose. It is about communicating decisiveness through timing and tone. When a corporation wavers between experimentation and execution, it invites doubt from stakeholders, employees, and executives. Decisive deployment signals direction. It tells the enterprise: this is not a trial balloon. This is the future. Behavioral science shows us that clarity reduces cognitive dissonance. When teams sense hesitation, they mirror it. When they see purpose, they align.

Why It Matters to Corporations: A corporation is a system of power, incentives, and status. Within this system, AI agents must be positioned because they do not simply "exist." And positioning requires decisiveness. An agent that is deployed with cautionary language ("we're just testing it out") will be treated like a fragile experiment. No one will bet their career on it. But an agent deployed with a confident statement ("we're using this to streamline policy issuance and drive faster underwriting") creates gravitational pull. From a political standpoint, decisive deployments permit functional leaders to align without fear of being left exposed. A hesitant rollout creates ambiguity, which in turn breeds delay. Think of the corporate middle as a series of gates. If leadership is ambiguous, the gates stay closed. If leadership is decisive, the gates swing open. There is also a financial case. Indecisiveness extends pilot phases, multiplies duplicative evaluations, and slows time-to-value. Corporations that deploy with hesitation incur opportunity costs. They pay twice, once for the tech and again for the time wasted on testing what should already be delivering value. Decisiveness leverages the principle of social proof. When people see a confident commitment to action, they interpret it as a signal of safety. They follow the signal. Agents that are rolled out with clear use cases, stakeholder commitments, and measurement plans earn legitimacy faster.

An executive stance, operational reinforcement, and accountability define purposeful deployment. It is this kind of purposeful deployment that generates traction. Deploying decisively is not about moving fast; it is about acting with clarity. In large enterprises, the difference between adoption and apathy often lies in the tone at the top. Decisive action creates alignment. Hesitation creates space for resistance. This principle is also about belief. When leadership speaks with conviction, teams believe. When leadership hedges, teams pause. Every deployment communicates more than a function. It communicates power. Decisiveness says, "We're not experimenting anymore. We're building." There are tactical benefits, too. A decisive rollout forces sharper change management, clearer training pathways, and firmer accountability structures. These are all ingredients that support long-term success. From an executive perspective, decisive deployment sets the tempo of transformation. It sends a signal across the organization: transformation is not optional. In practical terms, decisiveness can be organized into rollout plans: executive memos with clear statements, visual dashboards monitoring rollout stages, and KPIs integrated into performance management. These serve as tools for organizational signaling.

Real-World Example: A leading commercial bank intended to introduce an AI agent to support relationship managers with real-time insights during client meetings. The technology had been successfully tested, and the pilot was complete, but leadership hesitated. The deployment was referred to as a "continued evaluation phase." Adoption plateaued. Usage stagnated. Relationship managers were unsure if the tool was optional, temporary, or strategic. Six months later, the CIO revised the narrative. The agent was now positioned as a non-negotiable part of the relationship manager (RM) toolkit. Training was mandatory. KPIs were adjusted to include agent engagement. Messaging changed: "This is your advantage: use it or fall behind." The shift was immediate. Adoption jumped from 24% to 83% in one quarter. The only thing that changed was the decisiveness of the deployment. This example illustrates the power of commitment framing. When tools are offered tentatively, they are adopted in the same manner. This principle aligns with the commitment-consistency principle. People strive to act in line with their publicly stated commitments. By deploying agents with clear intent, organizations create a self-reinforcing cycle of adoption, reinforcement, and alignment. Deploy with purpose. Speak with conviction. Let the organization feel the resolve. Because in the power dynamics of enterprise change, decisiveness is the first domino.

Principle 6: Right Order, Right Time

Definition: Sequence Deployment Based on Organizational Readiness.

Principle 6 is not just about prioritization, it is also about sequencing political capital. In corporate environments, deploying the right agent too early, or in the wrong department, can kill momentum, invite resistance, and permanently brand AI as disruptive rather than enabling. This principle states that timing matters as much as capability. You must deploy agents in an order that aligns with the organization's cultural and political readiness. Organizational readiness is a blend of leadership sponsorship, team maturity, technological infrastructure, and change fatigue. Deploying an agent into a politically fragile team or under a skeptical leader is like trying to teach someone calculus before they understand multiplication. It gets swallowed. But sequenced properly, each deployment builds air cover for the next.

Why It Matters to Corporations: Organizations are not spreadsheets; they are organisms. Each division has a different level of maturity, leadership conviction, cultural climate, and power dynamics. This principle reminds us that deployment sequencing must be based on more than just technical feasibility. It must account for where the enterprise is most prepared to succeed and where early wins can be strategically leveraged. Too often, organizations deploy agents in high-impact areas before those areas are ready. Legal and compliance teams are typically risk-averse and politically cautious. Though promising for AI efficiency, they're not ideal for first deployments unless the teams are ready. Failure here not only halts progress but also tarnishes AI's reputation across the organization. It's better to start in departments with digital maturity, leadership support, and a readiness for change. Early wins in these areas provide proof of value, build momentum, attract supporters, and reduce skepticism.

The right deployment order is also about optics. A carefully managed rollout signals intentional, strategic progress. In contrast, a chaotic introduction breeds uncertainty and doubt. The enterprise watches not only what you do, but also the order in which you do it. From a behavioral science angle, this principle activates momentum. Small wins, strategically staged, build perceived inevitability. They create a cascading effect, in which each successful deployment increases the likelihood of the next one. Strategically, this principle invites you to look beyond the business case. Look at sponsor strength. Look at change fatigue. Look at integration complexity. Look at how the agent aligns with team culture. Success is never just about what the agent can do. It is about where it will thrive. In practical terms, apply this principle by building a readiness map. Score departments on data maturity, leadership support, prior automation success, and openness to change. Use that map to plot your sequence. Show the enterprise that deployment is reasoned, not random. From an influence perspective, this principle aligns with alliance building. The first success builds momentum for the next. Therefore, choosing the order of development and deployment is crucial to influence that progress.

Real-World Example: A global metals and mining company embarked on integrating AI agents throughout its operations, including mining, smelting, and logistics. The initial target was Finance, attracted by anticipated cost savings and efficiency. However, Finance's fragmented data environment and recent enterprise resource planning (ERP) changes had made the team wary, leading to staff experiencing fatigue and skepticism. Recognizing the risks, the transformation office assessed all business units for AI readiness. Mining Operations emerged as the best candidate, benefiting from robust leadership support, mature data infrastructure, and a culture open to innovation. The first deployment, a maintenance agent for autonomous equipment monitoring, was launched in this division. In just 90 days, it identified early signs of hydraulic pump failure on the haul-truck fleet, cutting downtime by 17% and extending asset life by six months. This achievement became an internal case study. The COO presented these results to the executive committee, highlighting improvements in cost and safety. The success changed company sentiment, prompting once-reluctant divisions to request AI solutions of their own. Six months later, as momentum built, the company rolled out a logistics optimization agent that employs predictive analytics to synchronize transportation with real-time output, a move embraced by the logistics division. The approach favored units ready for adoption and supported by leadership, ensuring initial wins set the stage for further progress. By the second year, with AI firmly established in operations and logistics, deployment expanded to Finance and Compliance. Notably, AI was recognized as a core strategic capability, and former skeptics sought involvement, citing practical gains.

Principle 6 emphasizes discipline. The desire to make a significant impact is strong. AI leaders aim for quick results, but patience is key in transformation. Sequencing deployments builds reputation and boosts momentum. If your first agent fails, it becomes the defining story. If it succeeds, it sets a new standard. Early wins not only deliver ROI but also generate political capital, enabling you to scale up in future efforts.

Principle 7: Scale in Stages

Definition: Deploy incrementally, too much too fast triggers rebellion.

Scaling AI agents requires more than technical implementation; it demands political, cultural, and psychological awareness. Organizations that attempt to scale AI initiatives all at once frequently face resistance, burnout, and instinctive pushback. Leaders must realize that if scaling is not rooted in demonstrated results and readiness, it will seem like an aggressive takeover. A phased approach, however, fosters trust, encourages adoption, and presents scaling as a strategic, well-managed process. In essence, scale must be achieved, not simply announced. Early pilots aren't solely technology tests; they act as a stage for organizational approval, signaling whether the company is ready for broader adoption. Even after success, expansion should be measured and controlled. You sequence. You build an agent growth curve that mirrors psychological readiness rather than just operational need.

Why It Matters to Corporations: Enterprises love to think in terms of scale. But scale, mismanaged, is chaos in disguise. The myth is that once something works in one area, it can be cloned across the enterprise. The reality is that organizational buy-in does not scale as easily as code. Every team has a different leadership structure, culture, tech stack, and appetite for change. This principle makes one truth plain: you do not scale trust, you earn it. When agents are pushed out too fast, adoption fractures. Teams resist the change because they were not part of the success story. Leaders question why they were not consulted, which in turn multiplies friction. People become spectators, not stakeholders. Scaling in stages allows each phase to create the case for the next. When the first few deployments succeed, they generate metrics, testimonials, and peer validation. When people see someone like them succeeding with an agent, they want in.

Principle 7 also acts as a risk containment mechanism. Early-stage agents provide signals: which workflows break, which resistance emerges, and which surprises arise. These serve as inputs for future rollouts. It is strategic iteration at scale. A common mistake made by enterprises is scaling by mandate. This triggers what psychologists call "reactance." Reactance is the instinctive resistance to being told what to do. But when you scale by invitation, you create a pull effect. Teams opt in because the agent is seen as a tool of empowerment, not control. Scaling in stages creates the illusion of inevitability, progressing slowly and then suddenly. And in power terms, there is nothing more compelling than a movement that feels organic yet orchestrated. Massive AI rollouts often overwhelm teams, threaten job security, and provoke political pushback. To maintain momentum, consider scaling as a strategic sequence rather than an overwhelming flood. You do not simply earn scale; you stage it. Approach each deployment as a referendum on trust, value, and organizational readiness. Many failed enterprise rollouts followed the "big bang" model, believing that more is better. However, most organizations cannot adapt to rapid, large-scale change. AI, given its potential to redefine workflows and challenge existing hierarchies, is particularly susceptible to internal resistance if deployed too quickly. When agents feel imposed, rather than welcomed, they quickly become scapegoats for issues they did not cause. Scaling in stages reflects strategic leadership, not just caution. By rolling out agents based on political receptivity and readiness, leaders secure early victories that pave the way for transformation. Early adopters become advocates, positive metrics accumulate, and organizational fear declines. See each stage as a soft referendum for a low-risk, high-reward chance to gain momentum and support. This approach not only de-risks transformation but also leverages every win as a source of power.

Real-World Example: A North American bank introduced AI agents by department, starting with loan origination. Each win earned trust and air cover, allowing them to expand. By the time Legal and Compliance joined, resistance was minimal. The genius of this approach lies not in its novelty but in its discipline. Rather than framing scale as a mandate, this bank treated it like a campaign. Every agent had a sponsor, a dashboard, and a defined impact zone. The loan origination team became the model, and their results were used in CEO town halls and board updates. Once the value was visible, demand was pulled from other departments rather than pushed. This is how agents earn legitimacy, not through promotion, but through performance. Scaling in stages also protects the program politically. If one department resists or underperforms, the broader agent strategy remains intact. This is asymmetric warfare for change agents, small wins that cascade into cultural change without drawing fire from skeptics. The goal is not to prove AI works. The goal is to prove that AI works in your business, using your metrics.

A European bank attempted to roll out a customer service AI agent across all business units at once. Despite strong pilot results in one unit, the full-scale launch met intense resistance. Different teams had different expectations. Some weren't trained. Others felt it was imposed. Within 90 days, usage dropped by 40%, and the rollout was paused. Contrast that with a North American bank that began in retail banking. The agent helped with the loan application pre-qualification. Once success metrics were shared, the loan cycle time dropped by 22%, customer complaints fell by 18%, and other business units took notice. The team then deployed the same agent in commercial banking, with slight customization. Once again, success. By the time the bank reached wealth management and operations, the agent had a reputation for being beneficial. Teams started to ask when they would get their version. The rollout was staged across 18 months, but by the end, agent usage was 7x higher than the failed "big bang" approach of its European counterpart. Scaling in stages not only protects you from failure but also manufactures demand. And in enterprise transformation, demand is the real accelerant.

You cannot scale what the organization has not yet metabolized. Principle 7 reminds us that transformation is not linear, but psychological. Each phase of a staged rollout involves not just deployment, but also persuasion and the building of momentum. Scaling in stages isn't about moving slowly; it's about acting intelligently. By treating each phase as a self-contained campaign, with proof, stories, and sponsorship, you turn scale into strategy. Instead of pushing change, you pull people in. You build an enterprise movement, one win at a time. From a behavioral science perspective, this principle employs pacing as a form of persuasion. People are more open to change when it feels predictable and reversible. A big-bang rollout removes these safeguards, while a staged deployment builds trust, reduces perceived risk, and enables adjustments. It makes success feel achievable. Corporations that scale too fast often leave a trail of resentment.

Teams feel coerced. Leaders feel bypassed. But when scale feels earned, the reaction is different. Teams feel proud. Leaders become champions. The AI program gains velocity because it is welcomed. This principle also builds institutional learning. Each rollout reveals something. That data is more than feedback; it is foresight used to sharpen the next phase. You create a continuous loop of progress. So scale, but scale in stages. Treat every deployment as a referendum. Let success vote for itself. Because the real power of AI agents is not just in what they can do, it is in how they are received within your organization.

Principle 8: Scale Without Spill

Definition: Scale with intent; do not let success breed chaos.

Success is seductive. Once an AI agent proves valuable, the urge to expand it quickly can shift careful strategy into chaos. Principle 8 cautions that momentum should not override intent: authentic progress must be protected, not compromised for the sake of fast scaling. When success is mismanaged, it leads to breakdowns instead of continued growth. This principle insists that expansion remains deliberate, even when demand soars. The term “spill” captures the turmoil when adoption outpaces governance, enthusiasm exceeds infrastructure, and teams introduce agents without adequate support. Left unchecked, scaling breeds disorder: agents develop inconsistently, data integrity is compromised, security risks grow, and user experience deteriorates. Scaling requires stewardship, not mere replication.

Why It Matters to Corporations: In high-performing enterprises, a successful AI deployment attracts fast followers. This is good, but only if the expansion is orchestrated. Uncontrolled scale fragments the agent ecosystem. It becomes harder to support, harder to secure, and harder to improve. Innovation becomes entropy. Corporations that fail to contain early-stage success often lose visibility into how agents are being used, modified, or integrated. Shadow implementations pop up. Variant codebases emerge. Different departments ask different vendors to “customize” their version. What began as a breakthrough becomes a burden. This is particularly dangerous in regulated industries like financial services, health care, and insurance. Uncoordinated scale creates exposure. Legal and compliance teams lose track of decision-making logic. Audit trails become murky, and the risk compounds.

From a behavioral science perspective, Principle 8 protects against optimism bias. Optimism bias is the tendency to underestimate the complexity of a task once early results are achieved. This often results in prematurely shifting from proof of concept to widespread adoption, a frequent pitfall in transformations. Scaling without a control plane doesn’t signify success but usually represents overconfidence. To avoid failure, set clear guardrails: define what “ready to scale” means, establish version-control policies, and leverage center-of-excellence models to distribute knowledge and maintain accountability. Think of early success as a cue to pause and stabilize, not speed up. Successful scaling should be orchestrated, not chaotic. The ideal state is one in which demand for agents rises, while supply is delivered with consistent quality, risk awareness, and support infrastructure.

From a power standpoint, this principle channels the concept of controlled influence. You want your success to speak for itself, and you also want to direct who listens, how it is interpreted, and what comes next. Scarcity can be a tool here. Instead of giving every department immediate access, create qualification criteria. Make departments "earn" the next phase by aligning with strategy, adopting data standards, or naming dedicated liaisons. This scarcity increases perceived value while ensuring readiness.

Real-World Example: A Fortune 100 manufacturer implemented a predictive maintenance agent on its factory floor, leveraging sensor data to predict machine failures and recommend preventative interventions. After one facility reported a 30% reduction in downtime, regional managers hurried to deploy the agent in their own plants. However, within 90 days, five distinct versions had appeared: some plants altered the logic engine, while others connected to different sensor data. This decentralized approach led to a loss of control and introduced errors. In one plant, a modified agent generated false positives, causing unnecessary shutdowns and resulting in millions of lost productivity. The CTO intervened, created a central governance council, and paused further deployment. The original team overhauled the model architecture to enable modular customization without fragmentation, enforced standardized APIs, and provided templates for plant-specific adjustments. Twelve months later, the agent was operational in over 50 locations, delivering consistent outcomes, unified dashboards, and a single source of truth. Order was reestablished, but at a price. The takeaway: success must be managed, or it can quickly devolve into chaos. Principle 8 reminds us to scale thoughtfully. Early wins in transformation programs can pose more risk than failure by prompting hasty replication. Scaling too soon or without proper oversight can create an ecosystem that outgrows its foundation. Organizations need a strategic approach beyond deployment that emphasizes governance to align infrastructure, security, and knowledge with rapid expansion. Building adaptable agent-operating models is vital for anticipating demand and managing complexity. This includes:

- Version control
- Governance councils
- Central documentation
- Deployment frameworks
- Training protocols for second-order users.

In transformation, momentum is only helpful if it is directional. Principle 8 ensures your AI momentum doesn't become mayhem. It safeguards scale from self-destruction. So when your agent succeeds, pause. Build the foundation that will allow that success to replicate with integrity. Because without clear intent, scaling up results in spills. And spilled progress is hard to clean up.

Chapter 1 Conclusion

The first step of any transformation sets the tone, conveying intent, discipline, and credibility. And AI adoption is no exception. Too often, enterprises stumble by making flashy announcements or rushing deployments, seeking innovation for its own sake. Chapter 1 reveals that strategy must precede spectacle: disciplined deployment is essential. Leaders who launch agents carelessly turn transformation into noise; those who act with precision create lasting advantages. Sequencing deployments where the enterprise is most prepared enables early wins that can be strategically leveraged. The chapter's eight principles, frank and demanding, identify the most common mistakes leaders make and form a clear manifesto for successful execution. Together, they draw a firm line between hype and genuine impact.

Chapter 2

Design Principles and Engineering Discipline

An agent's influence begins at design. The most powerful AI agent is not the one with the best algorithm; it is the one people trust, want to use, and do not need to be taught. Chapter 2 explores the architectural moves and behavioral science principles that make agents indispensable. These principles are not about feature sets; they are about psychological fidelity, trust signaling, and frictionless functionality. If Chapter 1 was about where and when to deploy, this chapter is about what you deploy, and whether it is built to be believed. Behind every effective AI agent is not just intelligence, but also emotional design. The most persuasive agents are engineered not simply to compute, but to convert. The enterprise landscape is littered with well-funded agents that failed to scale because they felt sterile, cold, or alien to the user. Behavioral science reminds us that people do not adopt what works best; they adopt what feels right. This chapter reframes design as persuasion, a continuous exercise in building trust, minimizing friction, and enhancing familiarity. When trust is built in, the agent sells itself. When it isn't, the enterprise will introduce paralyzing resistance. Design is not a downstream UI issue; it is the upstream foundation of influence and success.

Design is persuasion, a continuous exercise in building trust, minimizing friction, and enhancing familiarity.

DOI: 10.4324/9781003749899-4

Principle 9: Create Craveable Agents

Definition: Build agents that others want to use.

Craveability is the quality of an agent that makes people choose it when they don't have to. It combines three elements: effortless starts (zero learning curve), recognition routing (humans keep the credit), and a confidence boost (users feel more capable after each interaction). The principle avoids cluttering with features and instead emphasizes the moments that matter: "Can I do my task faster, with fewer errors, and feel in control?" Design cues include immediate usefulness without training, defaults set to assist (not ask), language that matches the user's own, and visible micro-wins (auto-filled fields, pre-checked compliance steps, one-click summaries). Agent-detected issues are safe and instructive and provide calibrated feedback. Personalization respects transparency. The interface remains humble: it integrates into existing tools, limits choices, and makes opting out simple. Craveable agents spread through attraction. They create advocates because they reduce grind in ways users can share with peers: "It saved me 20 minutes and caught the disclosure I would have missed." That message travels farther than any marketing material.

Why It Matters to Corporations: Adoption isn't a technical issue; it's a human one. An AI agent that isn't actively integrated into workflows will face political resistance, even if it works well. Behavioral science shows that people engage more with tools that feel familiar, effortless, and rewarding. This idea positions agents as something people want, not just something they are told to use. People don't resist AI; they resist friction, ego threats, and unfamiliar tools. Build for desire, not just compliance. Craveable agents sell themselves. The most successful corporate technologies aren't mandated; they're desired. Employees check their expense apps, productivity dashboards, or team messaging platforms not because they're forced to, but because those tools give them a sense of emotional or mental payoff. Craveability is the hidden engine behind adoption. Agents that garner daily engagement do so because they offer more than just functionality; they provide a feeling of fluency, control, or recognition and should be designed with that in mind. Agents must do more than reduce friction; they need to spark desire. Use behavioral hooks like variable rewards, personalized nudges, or mirrored mental models to embed agents into daily work routines. Wide-scale adoption requires more than permission; it demands desire. Mandates can start usage, but the real goal is to sustain it, especially across large, distributed teams. To do so, the following helps:

- **Discretionary use drives real outcomes.** Employees face endless demands. Tools that cause friction are quietly ignored. Desirable agents lower cognitive load. Processing fluency (information presented in familiar patterns) increases trust and speeds up decisions. Reducing effort encourages repeat use. Over time, discretionary use becomes standard; metrics change because people prefer the agent first.

- **Change fatigue is real.** After multiple transformations, the desire to learn "one more system" diminishes. Craveable agents seem like natural extensions of current workflows. No major training sessions needed. No new mental model required. The result: time-to-first-success measured in minutes, not weeks. That speed is highly valuable for sponsors facing adoption deadlines.
- **Labor relations and dignity.** In unionized or tightly regulated environments, the perception of agency matters. When agents handle tasks (rekeying, cross-checking, drafting) while humans focus on client moments and credit, resistance diminishes. The system feels supportive, not like surveillance. Complaints decrease; cooperation increases.
- **Frontline storytelling.** The most effective adoption campaign happens when a trusted peer says, "I use it because it helps." Social proof and messenger effects come into play: the right person, with a specific benefit, influences more behavior than a mass email ever could. Design for that moment by ensuring the agent provides immediate, clear relief.
- **Economic performance.** Craveability lowers training costs, support tickets, and rework. It also decreases churn: employees who feel competent and respected are less likely to leave. The CFO observes lower cost-to-serve; the CHRO sees higher engagement. The CISO encounters fewer workarounds because people no longer need shadow tools to get work done.
- **Brand and customer trust rely on customer-facing agents being highly appealing.** An excellent internal tool can be acceptable even if it's clunky; however, a great customer-facing tool must be seamless. When customers receive faster, kinder, more accurate service, they give credit to the people behind it. That's precisely what you want: humans in the spotlight, with the agent making that experience easier, safer, and more consistent.

Real-World Example: A regional commercial bank launched an assistant for relationship managers (RMs). Early usage lagged, and feedback was blunt: "It's clever, but it slows me down." The team rebuilt the tool for craveability with frontline RMs. Changes included a one-click brief before each client meeting (covering the last activity, risk flag, and one relevant insight), contextual follow-up drafting in the RM's tone, and compliance guardrails that autofilled disclosures with a soft confirmation. The UI mirrored the layout of the existing customer relationship management (CRM) tool; the agent appeared only when it could perform real work. Within three months, daily active use reached 88%. RMs reported saving 30–40 minutes per day, and complaint escalations fell by 19%. The team leader, who had warned against "robot managers," held a town hall acknowledging fewer late-day errors. Craveability centers on conversion. The change was not in the functionality itself, but in its presentation and how familiar it felt. The agent communicated in the users' language, mirrored their tone, anticipated their needs, and made them think the agent was part of their world. It wasn't intrusive; it was embraced. This demonstrates behavioral alignment: when a tool matches how people naturally think, work, and feel, adoption happens effortlessly. Senior leaders should ask their teams one question: *If your agent were optional, would people still choose it?* If not, you face a design failure, not a tech issue. To institutionalize:

- Design for the first minute, not the first month. Can a new user finish a fundamental task in 60 seconds?
- Make the agent carry the heavy work. Draft, reconcile, pre-check, and leave judgment and credit to humans.
- Write the sentence users will say. "It saved me X and helped me avoid Y." Build to make that accurate.
- Instrument micro-wins. Show saved steps, prevented errors, and time back – quietly.
- Keep the surface humble – fewer knobs, familiar patterns, easy exits.

Craveability is not fluff. It is the shortest path to sustained adoption and the cheapest insurance against program fatigue. When the tool feels like help and leaves the human with the win, the organization stops arguing about AI and starts using it every hour of every day.

Principle 10: Empathy by Design

Definition: Design for empathy before performance by establishing governance.

Innovation without empathy is merely efficiency without trust. Clients and executives do not adopt tools they do not trust, even if those tools function well. Behavioral triggers like transparency, confirmation cues, and error-handling rituals help build subconscious trust. The most powerful AI agents are often the ones users trust before they fully understand them. Function follows faith. Designing with empathy heuristics from the start helps your agent earn a seat at the table. In behavioral economics, trust is built faster through empathetic design than through performance alone. People don't audit algorithms; they look for trust signals. Eye-tracking studies reveal that simple confirmations, transparent logic paths, and predictable UI behavior all create micro-moments of trust. This is particularly true for AI, where most users cannot evaluate accuracy, but everyone can easily detect inconsistency.

Design becomes a proxy for integrity. When users feel an agent understands and respects their decision-making environment, they are more likely to rely on it. Before a single line of code is written, an AI agent needs its governing rules, boundaries, and escalation protocols defined in detail. Governance is a fundamental part of design. Governance isn't an afterthought; without it, even the most advanced agent can become a liability, a compliance risk, or a political issue. In corporate contexts, ambiguity equals risk. Agents running without clear governance structures risk uncontrolled changes, inconsistent actions, and reputational damage. Establishing operational rules, decision-making boundaries, data access permissions, and audit requirements before starting technical work ensures the agent stays within the parameters that leadership has approved. This isn't about slowing down innovation, but about promoting safe, credible adoption. Governance guardrails give business stakeholders the confidence to scale technology and make development easier with clear, stable parameters. When governance precedes development, the result is an AI agent that is functional, trustworthy, politically defensible, and legally resilient.

Why It Matters to Corporations: Enterprises don't fail at AI adoption because they lack talented engineers. AI adoption often fails because it overlooks governance considerations early on, leading to rework, delayed launches, or outright cancellations. Incorporating governance from the start ensures the agent's operating model complies with regulations without costly redesigns. Executives are more likely to support agents who have an approved governance framework. It shows that risks have been assessed and managed through clear operational rules, making it easier to present the project to the board. Agents operating under a consistent governance model can scale faster and integrate smoothly with existing enterprise systems. Teams understand expectations, risk management teams know how to monitor, and end users trust the reliability of the outcomes.

Real-World Example: A multinational insurance company aimed to build a claims triage agent. Initially, an innovation lab created a prototype using a generative model to summarize and classify claims. While technically impressive, critical gaps emerged: no escalation process, no explainability framework, and no record-keeping protocol. When compliance reviewed the tool, rollout was halted. Because there was no pre-approved governance model, each control had to be added after the fact, delaying deployment by nine months and necessitating a rebuild of some features. In the next attempt, the company changed tactics, assembling a cross-functional governance council before any coding began. This group set clear decision boundaries (the agent could classify, but not approve high-value claims), created audit trails (with every recommendation logged and justified), and required human oversight for flagged risks. With these protocols in place from the outset, development proceeded without friction. Compliance was achieved on the first try. The agent launched in under six months and was quickly scaled to new regions. This shows that governance isn't a bureaucratic burden but a driver of speed, scale, and trust. By setting rules before coding, you ensure fewer compliance delays, faster expansion through repeatable frameworks, and greater stakeholder confidence thanks to embedded oversight and accountability.

In AI transformation, speed matters, as does survival. And survival depends on trust. Trust is earned when leadership can say with certainty: *We know precisely how this agent behaves, where it draws its boundaries, and how it will be monitored.* Follow this principle rigorously. Let empathy be the architect of your build; otherwise, it will be engineered empty without trust.

Principle 11: Choreograph the Unmissable Moment

Definition: Showcase an emotionally resonant win.

The premise in Principle 4 is to start in stealth mode, and once you gain momentum with successful agents being deployed and adding value to your firm, it is time to create deliberate theater that forges a memory and sets the standard. Choreograph one unmissable moment: a tangible, emotionally resonant win that maps to a value-based outcome. The kind of experience people talk about after the meeting. It is the executive demo that lands in 90 seconds and leaves the room aligned. It is the field trial that makes frontline staff pull out their phones to record. It blends the peak-end rule (people remember the best moment and the ending) with social proof (people follow what peers praise) and salience (what stands out gets stored). Think a claims agent settling a low-risk case live in 20 seconds with policy references; a sales agent answering the client's hidden objection with sourced evidence; a planning agent collapsing a five-day forecast cycle to minutes while citing the CFO's target bands. The choreography of Principle 11 is purposeful: you showcase safety, speed, and status (the user looks competent, not replaced). You wrap it in authority (sponsor in the room, risk pre-cleared) and scarcity (limited invitation, specific cohort). You stage the story: before/after, 1–2 charts, one internal testimonial. Then you end on the ask, a concrete next step that converts awe into action. The alignment shows that the agent supports the business humans already care about, and you grant permission for others to follow. In crowded enterprises, movements start in the same way: with a moment people can point to and say, "That." The main difference between Principles 4 and 11 is timing. Principle 4 suggests deploying your first agent into the enterprise silently, giving leaders time to learn, refine, and control the narrative. But once that first agent is on a good adoption path, it is time to implement Principle 11 and choreograph the unmissable moment.

Why It Matters to Corporations: Enterprises are attention economies. Competing initiatives, tight calendars, and political risk mean you get a tiny window to set the narrative. If your first agent arrives as just another tool, it gets lost in the noise. If it comes as a moment, it becomes a reference point: "Do it like that." Choreographing the unmissable moment works because it compresses proof and permission into one act:

- **Proof:** You demonstrate the outcome, live, on the metric that matters (time, revenue, risk), leveraging video media.
- **Permission:** With the sponsor present and risk already briefed, the room gets a meta-signal: "This is safe to support."

Behaviorally, the choreography fixes three problems:

1. **Status Threat:** If the demo portrays the human as strong, making fast decisions and explicit judgments, middle managers will not feel displaced. They feel amplified. That reduces covert resistance.
2. **Ambiguity:** People infer enterprise priority from production value. A polished, tight, sponsor-led moment telegraphs importance and inevitability. A scrappy demo telegraphs "maybe."
3. **Memory:** The peak-end rule says people remember the high point and how it ended. Design both: a killer on-task moment, what the early tech world would call a "killer feature," and a crisp close with a specific next step and timebox.

Choreographed spectacle also earns comms oxygen: intranet stories, town-hall clips, and CEO all-hands shout-outs. Those are not vanity; they are distribution. Internal fame turns into a pipeline: teams start asking for the agent rather than dodging it. Add scarcity ("We're opening three additional cohorts this quarter on a first-come, first-served basis") and you replace push with pull. "We did one 12-minute showpiece with the COO. The phone did not stop for a week," – VP Operations, Global logistics leader. Finally, spectacle shortens sales cycles with control functions. When Risk, Legal, and Security see that the showpiece adheres to policy and logs itself impeccably, their first answer shifts from "no" to "yes, with conditions." You've preempted objections on stage.

Real-World Example: A Fortune 200 U.S. manufacturer and equipment solutions provider began discreetly implementing AI agents in its supply chain and field operations. Early successes remained confined within departments, such as maintenance agents predicting motor failures two weeks ahead and scheduling agents boosting uptime. The CIO and COO realized that quiet achievements alone would not drive company-wide adoption; a decisive moment was needed. This breakthrough arrived at its Annual Operations Leadership Summit, attended by 300 plant managers and divisional VPs. There, they unveiled a digital planning agent that reduced production forecasting time from 5 days to just 45 minutes. The demonstration focused on a common pain point: slow responses to unexpected downtimes and urgent customer orders. Their goal was to showcase a real-time transformation in under two minutes. Collaborating with the transformation office, the CIO orchestrated a clear, impactful demo that displayed the dashboards and highlighted the customer impact and margin protection, all aligned with the CFO's efficiency goals. The COO declared, "This is not a pilot. This is how we'll plan our plants next quarter." The crowd applauded. The event quickly went viral internally. Within 48 hours, it was featured on the intranet and spotlighted by the CEO. Executives shared the story at investor and town hall meetings. Interest in AI soared by 300%, attracting even traditionally reluctant groups such as procurement, compliance, and finance. The demonstration provided both concrete evidence and organizational buy-in to advance AI adoption. A simple playbook:

- Choose a pain everyone respects – settlement cycle time, underwriting turnaround, quarter-end close.
- Script a single unforgettable moment – not ten features, one outcome.
- Put risk on stage – how the safety valve, the audit stamp, the known limits.
- Close with a commitment – "Three more cohorts. Applications due Friday."

Principle 12: Make It Mission Infrastructure

Definition: Treat your ai agent ecosystem like critical infrastructure, not a side project.

This principle reframes agents from being "innovations to try" into critical systems to depend on. Just as you wouldn't roll out a payment network, compliance database, or ERP system without uptime guarantees, maintenance budgets, and clear ownership, you should not deploy AI agents without embedding them into the mission-critical backbone of the enterprise. Mission infrastructure means the agent is:

- **Resilient:** Built for redundancy and failover.
- **Measurable:** Monitored with real-time KPIs tied to business outcomes.
- **Owned:** Supported by clear accountability, service level agreements (SLAs), and operational funding.

Critically, this infrastructure is foundational to delivering on the 4Rs introduced earlier: risk, revenue, resilience, and relationships, the core outcomes agents are expected to drive. Without it, agents remain experimental; with it, they become indispensable.

When agents live on the periphery, they suffer "pilot purgatory," wherein they are tolerated as experiments but ignored in workflows. When they are integrated as essential infrastructure, they get the same executive protection, budget stability, and operational rigor as the systems they enhance or replace. If you don't institutionalize AI agents as infrastructure now, you will be structurally outpaced by competitors who do. The market rewards organizations that integrate AI into their operations early. Everyone else is condemned to play catch-up from a position of weakness.

Why It Matters to Corporations: Focusing on infrastructure is not just an IT decision; it is a strategic positioning move. Once something is "infrastructure," removing it requires a formal decommissioning process. That permanence changes how users perceive and interact with it. Ultimately, the shift to mission infrastructure is about ensuring your agent not only survives but thrives, scales, and becomes invisible in the best way—so integrated into daily operations that people forget there was ever another way to work.

- **Stability Builds Trust:** If users believe the agent is experimental, they'll hesitate to rely on it for mission-critical tasks. Positioning it as infrastructure signals permanence, a psychological cue that the system is here to stay. This also reassures investors, regulators, and partners that the capability is embedded in the company's operational DNA.
- **Operational Funding and Governance:** Pilots are often funded with discretionary budgets that dry up in a downturn. Infrastructure receives operational budgets that are predictable and protected, funding streams that allow for continuous improvement, and the embedding of agents as infrastructure forces that lead to long-term resource commitment.
- **Risk Management and Resilience:** Infrastructure-level systems are built for redundancy, security, and compliance. Agents treated this way undergo the same rigorous testing, contingency planning, and monitoring as other core systems. This dramatically reduces the likelihood of catastrophic outages, security breaches, or compliance violations.
- **Executive Visibility:** When agents are classified as infrastructure, they naturally become part of executive dashboards, strategic reviews, and board discussions. That visibility not only drives accountability but also opens the door to strategic expansion into new business areas.
- **Political Permanence:** In large organizations, what gets classified as "core" gets protected. By moving your agents into that category, you insulate them from leadership changes, budget cycles, and shifting innovation trends.

Real-World Example: A Fortune 50 logistics company piloted an AI agent to optimize last-mile delivery routes. Initially, the system was treated as an "innovation lab experiment" and ran in parallel to legacy routing software. Results were good. There were 7% cost savings in the first quarter, but adoption plateaued because regional managers viewed it as optional. The turning point came when the CIO moved the agent into the same operational category as ERP and fleet management systems. This triggered:

- A 24/7 monitoring team with defined escalation protocols.
- Full integration into driver handheld devices, replacing old routing tools.
- SLAs guaranteeing 99.9% uptime.
- Board-level KPIs for delivery efficiency that are directly tied to the agent's performance.

Adoption reached 100% within six months, resulting in a 14% increase in cost savings. Notably, regional managers no longer debated whether to use the agent; it became the company's standard operating procedure. The resilience of mission infrastructure separates fragile, champion-dependent initiatives from those that survive leadership changes, budget cuts, and tech trends. By embedding your AI ecosystem at the heart of operations, you safeguard it from the instability that often derails innovations. Practically, adopting this approach involves:

- Classifying the agent as a vital part of the enterprise's mission-critical systems.
- Allocating operational (not experimental) budgets for its entire lifecycle and subjecting it to the same governance, testing, and resilience standards as other essential systems.
- Including it in enterprise-wide reports and executive dashboards.

Principle 13: Design for Limits

Definition: Architect the operating model around strategic constraints.

Based on the idea that constraints are not disadvantages, limits enhance design decisions and help control complexity. In AI agent development, "Design for Limits" involves intentionally specifying what the agent will not do, how it will behave under pressure, and where it will defer to human judgment. Limits extend beyond technical aspects such as data volume, processing speed, or uptime. They also include governance rules, ethical boundaries, compliance obligations, and political realities inside the organization. By embedding these limits into the architecture from the start, you avoid uncontrolled sprawl, role confusion, and stakeholder backlash. An agent with no clear boundaries becomes a liability technically, operationally, and politically. An agent designed with explicit limits becomes a trusted specialist, known for reliability rather than overreach.

Why It Matters to Corporations: Enterprise AI rollouts often fail not because of poor performance, but because of scope creep and governance failure. When agents are allowed to expand capabilities without explicit boundaries, they drift into domains where they are less effective, create compliance and audit exposure, and step on other teams' toes, triggering political resistance.

- **Corporate Politics and Trust:** A well-defined limit communicates to stakeholders that the agent will not "eat their job" or intrude on their turf. This is especially important in large corporations where role boundaries are power boundaries. By declaring, for example, "This agent will only handle Tier-1 customer service queries and escalate all others," you reduce defensive pushback.
- **Operational Resilience:** Systems designed without limits often fail catastrophically under extreme load because they're expected to "handle

anything." Designing for limits allows you to predict, test, and manage edge cases rather than being blindsided by them.

- **Compliance and Risk:** In regulated industries, limits are your shield. By integrating these measures into the architecture, such as restricting data access and prohibiting unsupervised decision-making in high-stakes areas, you instill confidence in regulators and compliance teams from the outset.
- **Engineering Discipline:** Clear limits help prioritize effectively. Instead of pursuing every possible feature, teams concentrate on capabilities that provide the highest value within the scope. This often speeds up time-to-market and minimizes technical debt.

Real-World Example: A multinational insurance company deployed a claims-processing agent. In the initial pilot, the agent was allowed to process any claim type regardless of complexity – auto, health, and/or property. Within six months, error rates spiked, compliance flagged multiple violations, and the human adjusters began actively bypassing the tool. In the redesign, leadership applied "Design for Limits":

- The agent was restricted to handling auto claims under $5,000 with no injury reports.
- All other cases were routed automatically to a human adjuster.
- The agent's UI made the limit visible: "This claim is outside my scope. Routing to an adjuster."

Within three months, error rates decreased by 72%, compliance violations dropped to zero, and adjusters reported greater trust in the system. Adoption grew naturally because the tool became more predictable and reliable. "Design for Limits" emphasizes psychology as much as engineering. In the corporate world, trust is valuable, and nothing builds trust faster than consistent behavior. By clearly defining and respecting boundaries, your AI agents send a message: I know my lane, and I stay in it. From a strategic standpoint, this principle also preserves political capital. Every team, every department, and every executive has invisible lines they do not want crossed. When your agent respects those lines by design, you avoid the political traps that sink so many enterprise initiatives. In practice, applying this principle means:

- Mapping the operational, compliance, and political boundaries during design, not after deployment.
- Building graceful failover pathways for scenarios outside the limit.
- Communicating the agent's limits clearly to users helps them understand what to expect.

Counterintuitively, limits can also accelerate expansion. By succeeding within a clearly defined scope, you establish a foundation of trust that encourages stakeholders to expand capabilities later. In short, limits are not a cage; they are a launchpad.

Principle 14: Invisible Integration

Definition: Design agents that blend seamlessly into existing workflows.

The most effective AI agents integrate smoothly into the workflow. They don't force people to learn a new interface, remember new login details, or give up the tools they already rely on. Instead, they work within existing applications, channels, and processes employees use daily, quietly improving capabilities without disrupting routines. Invisible integration aims to make your AI agent so seamless that users barely notice where the human ends and the agent begins. This approach relies on behavioral inertia: people naturally stick with what's familiar, and the more friction you add, the more resistance you encounter. Integration is not just technical; it's psychological and strategic. An agent that integrates invisibly avoids political pushback from leaders protective of their current systems. It turns skeptics into quiet supporters because they don't have to "switch systems," and they see their work becoming faster, easier, and more precise without conscious effort.

Why It Matters to Corporations: Invisible integration drives frictionless adoption. Every additional click, login, or workflow change erodes adoption rates. Agents that surface in familiar environments, such as a CRM dashboard, Slack thread, or Excel spreadsheet, bypass this drop-off entirely. Integration, when done right, can reduce change management costs. The most significant hidden cost in digital transformation is training. When agents integrate invisibly, you eliminate or drastically reduce the need for structured onboarding. This is especially critical in large organizations where thousands of employees would otherwise require training. Invisible integration also provides the following benefits:

- **Preserves Core System Investments:** CIOs and CTOs have spent years and millions building core enterprise systems. An AI agent that layers on top rather than replacing those systems ensures ROI is protected while still enabling transformation.
- **Accelerates Time-to-Impact:** By embedding into existing workflows, agents start producing measurable results almost immediately after launch. There's no lag time for user adaptation, no parallel systems, and no risk of "shadow processes" emerging.
- **Minimizes Organizational Resistance:** Cultural resistance often hinders AI projects more than technical issues. An unseen approach avoids triggering the political immune system. Instead of announcing, "Here's a new AI tool you must use," you quietly provide employees with a better version of the tools they already trust.

Real-World Example: A Fortune 100 chemicals company needed a predictive maintenance system for its plant operations. At first the IT department considered creating a standalone portal where plant managers could log in, run diagnostics, and review results. Unsurprisingly, the pilot had low adoption. The breakthrough came when the team re-engineered the agent to directly integrate with the supervisory control and data acquisition (SCADA) control screens that managers already used. Alerts appeared in the same interface as other system notifications, and clicking them opened contextual recommendations without leaving the control view. Adoption soared to 97% within the first month. Unplanned downtime decreased by 18%, saving $24M annually. No formal training was needed; the integration built on existing familiarity with the system, making adoption natural. Invisible integration is a political and behavioral strategy disguised as a technical choice. You are not just embedding APIs; you are embedding change that avoids resistance and speeds up impact. Applying this principle requires:

- **Mapping High-Traffic Workflows:** Identify where users spend the most time and meet them there.
- **Prioritizing API-First Architecture:** Build agents to plug into multiple endpoints without forcing workflow rewrites.
- **Leveraging Familiar User Interface/User Experience (UI/UX) Patterns:** Adopt visual and interaction patterns users already know.
- **Partnering with System Owners Early:** Secure buy-in from those who control critical infrastructure platforms to prevent integration blockers.

The underlying behavioral principle is *status quo bias*. People tend to prefer familiar systems, even when new ones promise better performance. Invisible integration uses that bias to its advantage, making the agent appear as a natural extension of the status quo rather than a challenge to it. Key takeaway: the less the user notices your AI agent as a "separate tool," the more likely it is to be used and the more likely your AI transformation will succeed without costly culture battles.

Principle 15: Zero-Learning Curve

Definition: Design agents that just work, no training required.

A zero-learning curve is not a luxury; it is a basic requirement. When agents use familiar metaphors from current work tools, the risk of rejection drops. Teams feel more confident, more in control, and more likely to engage. Agents that need onboarding become organizational liabilities. Those that require no instruction turn into political assets. The best agent training manual is no manual at all.

Why It Matters to Corporations: Training hampers adoption. Agents must "show up fluent," anticipate intent, mirror interface norms, and require no explanation. In behavioral science, cognitive fluency builds user confidence. This principle ensures your agent gains trust by being frictionless. If training is needed to use your agent, you've already lost the first political battle. Fluent design is strong. Cognitive fluency is a powerful predictor of perceived competence. The easier something is to use, the more we believe it works. This is especially important in agent design. The user experience should not demand effort; it must provide clarity. Interfaces should mirror existing tools, workflows should feel natural, and every interaction should lessen decision fatigue. This is not just good user experience; it's a strategic use of behavioral science.

Real-World Example: A global metals and mining company developed an AI agent to optimize ore hauling and fleet dispatch across its open-pit operations. Anticipating resistance from supervisors and operators accustomed to familiar protocols, the design team integrated the agent seamlessly into the existing fleet management dashboard, preserving button placement, color scheme, and command structure. Rather than overhaul the interface, they added a context-aware suggestion layer that offered real-time route adjustments, maintenance alerts, and shift optimizations, all in the long-established visual format. No separate login or new training was required. Within two weeks, operator adoption soared over 95%, as supervisors embraced the subtle upgrade. Cycle times improved by 8%, unplanned maintenance fell by 12%, and dispatch reliability increased globally. Importantly, the rollout saw zero operational friction, no learning curve, and no productivity loss. By embedding the AI agent in a way that felt natural, the company converted potential resistance into enthusiastic endorsement. Employees trusted the agent for its intuitiveness, which led to higher data quality and smarter operations. Thus, a quiet digital enhancement became a worldwide standard, proving that in industrial environments, innovation works best when it goes unnoticed.

Chapter 2 Conclusion

Design is not aesthetics; it is persuasion. Each interaction with an agent either builds trust or breeds rejection. The most innovative model fails if it feels foreign. Design your agents as though the user is skeptical—because they are. Design is your first and best defense against organizational resistance. AI agents don't succeed by dazzling users. They grow by dissolving skepticism. The architecture of your agent should assume users have been burned before, by legacy systems, failed pilots, or overpromised dashboards. Build trust into the layout by leveraging empathy. Build want (desire) into the workflow. When you design with persuasion and empathy in mind, your agent becomes a trusted extension of the user. In AI, design is destiny. The truth: design is not decoration. Too many corporate AI initiatives stumble because design is treated as a cosmetic afterthought, a "nice to have" polish applied after engineers declare the code ready. But in an enterprise context, design is the primary obstacle to influence. An agent that feels alien will be resisted no matter how capable it is. Conversely, an agent that feels natural, aligns with existing workflows, is embedded invisibly into decision cycles, and signals reliability earns political capital with every use. These principles transform an agent from "the new tool IT wants you to try" into "the way things are done here."

Chapter 1 was about the discipline of *where* and *when* to deploy; Chapter 2 is about *what* you deploy and, more importantly, how it feels to the people who must use it. Technology succeeds or fails not in code, but in adoption. An AI agent that is powerful yet unloved, elegant yet mistrusted, will gather dust. An agent that is simple, craveable, and trusted becomes indispensable. The principle of this chapter is timeless: **form follows function**. Build agents people *want* to use, and adoption takes care of itself. These principles collectively form a design doctrine, signaling to leaders that AI agents are more than technical assets; they represent products, experiences, and the organization's intentions. Design is not just a luxury in enterprise transformation; it is crucial for establishing credibility and trust. The stakes are high. If agents are designed poorly, the consequences go beyond wasted investment. Employees lose trust in leadership. Frontline adoption falters. Skepticism spreads. Regulatory scrutiny intensifies. Conversely, when agents are designed with craveability, empathy, trust, and invisible integration, they become viral inside the organization. Adoption grows organically. Resistance melts. Agents shift from novelties to necessities. Design principles are, at their core, persuasion principles. A craveable agent persuades employees to use it. A showpiece persuades leaders to fund it. Infrastructure persuades regulators to trust it. Zero-learning curve persuades skeptics to give it a chance. The act of design is the act of influence. Within is a political playbook for design, illustrating to leaders that every choice conveys a message about what the first agent looks like, how it integrates, what it promises, and how it fails. Each principle ensures that the message builds adoption rather than resistance. The truth is simple: enterprises don't scale agents because the algorithms work. They scale because the people who use them trust them, enjoy them, and demand them.

Persona Highlights

Jordan, Chief Strategy & Transformation Officer

- Needs to "Create Craveable Agents" with trust-centered design to prove adoption is sustainable.
- *Key takeaway:* First, agents must serve as showpieces that accelerate the credibility of transformation.

Claire, Chief Financial Officer

- Sees “Design for Limits” as a guardrail against overspending and runaway complexity.
- *Key takeaway:* Agents must be built as infrastructure, but with financial discipline.

Rafael, Chief Technology Officer

- Anchors on “Make It Mission Infrastructure” and “Invisible Integration.”
- *Key takeaway:* Agents must blend seamlessly into enterprise architecture as core systems do.

Simone, Chief Human Resources Officer

- Values craveability and a “Zero-Learning Curve” as critical to workforce trust.
- *Key takeaway:* Agents must empower employees emotionally as much as functionally.

Mo, Chief Marketing Officer

- Energized by “Choreograph the Unmissable Moment.”
- *Key takeaway:* The first deployment must be staged as a story of innovation that excites the enterprise and signals brand leadership.

Chapter 3

Economic Justification and Return on Investment

AI agents do not earn survival by technical brilliance; they earn it by economic indispensability. In corporations, every new system competes for resources, attention, and executive sponsorship. This chapter focuses on the principles that anchor AI agents in cold, hard outcomes. The goal is simple: make the agent too valuable to cut. Using behavioral cues like loss aversion, visualized ROI, and effort-reduction framing, these principles equip leaders to frame AI agents not as experiments but as financial instruments that improve performance, reduce costs, and reveal hidden upside.

An AI agent that cannot justify itself will not survive the boardroom. In global enterprises, credibility isn't a by-product of code. Clean data, sound economics, and a transparent chain from input-to-impact earn it. This chapter makes a simple promise: if you fix the process, surface the truth, sell the ease, quantify the gains, justify the spend, and report reality without spin, your agents will move from experiment to engine. The opposite is just as true. Automating a broken workflow can lead to the industrialization of waste. Hide the evidence trail, and you inflame politics. Confuse effort with outcome, and you will lose budget when the cycle turns.

Executives do not buy AI; they buy risk-adjusted results.

Executives do not buy AI; they buy risk-adjusted results. This is why the principles within Chapter 3 speak the language of CFOs, COOs, and chief risk officers. We focus on the order of operations ("Fix First, Then Automate"), the experience promise ("Effortless is Everything"), the financial narrative ("Reveal Hidden ROI_2"), the investment standard ("Prove the Return"), Human-to-Agent measurement ("Govern the Future"), and the integrity of reporting ("Mirror,

DOI: 10.4324/9781003749899-5

Not Mask"). Each principle blends behavioral science with operational discipline so the numbers tell a story people can trust and act on. The narrative that follows is blunt on purpose. In large organizations, good intentions are cheap and political gravity is strong. These principles help you set a higher bar: cleaner baselines, clearer causality, faster wins, and dashboards that withstand audit. The goal is not a prettier pilot. The goal is a durable, defensible operating model where agents make work easier, improve economics, and make truth more available without turning every improvement into a referendum on who was right or wrong.

Principle 16: Fix First, Then Automate

Definition: Do not automate a broken process.

The temptation to automate quickly is strong. Technology dazzles executives, budgets are allocated for transformation, and leadership craves visible progress. But when automation is layered on dysfunction, it does not produce efficiency; instead, it amplifies inefficiency at scale. A flawed process, filled with bottlenecks, redundancies, or outdated logic, cannot be fixed by simply adding an AI agent. Instead, it must be examined, simplified, and strengthened before automation is considered. This principle establishes a discipline: fix first, then automate. It requires leaders to face the uncomfortable truths about their organization's workflows. Where are the delays? Where is the wasted effort? Which steps exist not because they add value but because they once addressed an older problem? AI agents perform best when the system around them is coherent, streamlined, and logical. They falter under the burden of inherited complexity. A company that automates chaos does not improve intelligence; it cultivates confusion. Conversely, a company that intentionally redesigns workflows with clarity creates an environment where AI agents can generate exponential value, an actual return on intelligence. The lesson is simple but powerful: automation is not a cure for dysfunction. It acts as an amplifier. And amplification, when applied to disorder, only increases noise.

Why It Matters to Corporations: Automating flawed processes rarely improves efficiency; it simply magnifies the underlying issues, increasing organizational vulnerability. That's why it's essential to fix processes before automating them. At the operational level, automation applied to unresolved processes creates structural weaknesses. AI systems and agents need clear, consistent, logical workflows to succeed. When automation is introduced into ambiguous or redundant processes, it accelerates existing problems rather than solving them. Errors proliferate, exceptions become more common, and business continuity suffers. Issues that were previously manageable through human judgment or workarounds become systemic and hidden, surfacing only when disruptions occur.

Far from achieving efficiency, automating chaos makes systems more fragile and prone to collapse as they scale. The financial implications are severe; automation requires significant investment in technology, talent, integration, and change management. Investing in broken processes entrenches inefficiencies, increases costs, frustrates customers, and results in failed projects with sunk costs. The transformation narrative collapses when ROI is based on dysfunctional foundations. Culturally, automation used as a superficial fix erodes employee trust and engagement. Staff easily spot when automation is deployed without fundamental process redesign, leading to skepticism and resistance. This negative sentiment can spread, hindering future automation efforts and making it hard to rebuild trust. However, when processes are streamlined first, AI agents become natural, effective extensions of work, quickly delivering tangible value and facilitating smooth adoption.

Fixing process issues before automation brings strategic benefits: enhanced employee adoption, reduced costs, and avoidance of automating inefficiencies. Clear workflows clarify roles, support workforce redesign, and generate cleaner data for better AI recommendations. Leading with process repair improves efficiency, agility, and the ability to measure AI impact. This method inspires stakeholder trust. As regulators increase AI oversight, particularly in sensitive sectors, demonstrating process optimization demonstrates strong governance. Investors value companies that combine discipline and speed. In contrast, automating broken processes risks employee resistance and reputational damage if customer problems persist.

Scarcity sharpens the urgency of this principle. Competitors are not waiting. They are already fixing their processes, embedding orchestration capability, and moving quickly to deploy agents into workflows that make sense. Every quarter that passes without this discipline narrows the time window for differentiation. Once competitors achieve parity, catching up requires disproportionately higher investment. Fixing processes after others have automated theirs means fighting uphill against both perception and momentum.

Executives are stewards of capital and credibility.

Finally, this principle directly addresses leadership responsibility. Executives are stewards of capital and credibility. Addressing issues before automating demonstrates stewardship of both. It signals to the workforce that transformation is about real substance, not just performance. It also reassures markets that investments in AI are made with purpose, not haste. And it reassures regulators that governance is embedded in the transformation's DNA, not applied retroactively after failures occur.

For a corporation, then, the importance of this principle cannot be overstated. Fixing before automating is not a delay tactic. It is not hesitation or risk aversion. It is sequencing done correctly. It is the recognition that automation is an amplifier, not a cure, and that what it amplifies must be worthy of scale. Those who honor this discipline will find themselves compounding value year after year. Those who ignore it will discover, too late, that they have invested millions in automating fragility. In the end, this principle asks a simple question of leaders: Do you want to scale excellence or scale dysfunction? The answer to that question determines whether automation becomes a strategic asset or an expensive liability.

Real-World Example: Consider a leading global logistics provider. The company tried to automate its shipment-tracking process, believing that AI-powered automation would reduce manual reconciliation. The problem was that the underlying process was broken: data came from multiple unaligned systems, with inconsistent formats and manual overrides. When the automation went live, the AI agent amplified flaws, leading to incorrect entries, confusing customers with conflicting updates, and causing costly manual escalations. Customer complaints doubled in the first quarter, and the expected efficiency gains disappeared. The company paused. Instead of abandoning AI entirely, leadership adopted a new approach: fix issues first, then automate. They began a process redesign by merging data sources, standardizing field names, and removing redundant approval steps. Only then did they restart the agent. This time, the results were impressive: tracking accuracy rose to 98%, customer complaints fell by 40%, and manual escalations dropped by 70%. The lesson was clear: the problem wasn't the technology but the process. By fixing the foundation before scaling the solution, the company turned chaos into clarity, and automation became a booster, not a burden.

Representing one of the most essential disciplines in corporate AI transformation, this principle demands patience in a world that celebrates speed. It asks executives to value clarity over theater, to embrace redesign before scale, and to understand that automation is not a cure but a catalyst on the quest for a return on intelligence.

- **Automation amplifies.** It will amplify efficiency when paired with strong processes and inefficiency when paired with weak ones.
- **Fixing first creates legitimacy.** Employees and customers alike recognize when an AI agent has been deployed into a system that makes sense. This recognition builds trust and accelerates adoption.
- **Long-term ROI depends on discipline.** Shortcuts may deliver short-term optics, but they rarely create sustainable value. Fixing processes before automating them ensures that AI agents generate compounding returns, not collapsing ones.

In behavioral science, this principle draws on authority, social proof, and scarcity. Leaders earn authority by investing in process redesign before agent deployment. Social proof is provided by industry examples showing measurable gains from this approach. Scarcity motivates action: the chance to optimize before competitors automate is short. Once others do, catching up is more expensive. This isn't about slowing progress but sequencing it correctly. Fixing before automating is not hesitation; it is precision.

Those who embrace this principle will find their agents are not only effective but also enduring. Those who ignore it will one day face the sobering truth: they have automated themselves into a state of fragility. Fix first. Then automate. That is how leaders turn AI from spectacle into substance, from cost into compounding advantage.

Principle 17: Effortless Is Everything

Definition: The promise of effortless execution.

The promise of AI agents lives or dies on a single perception: how easy it feels to achieve value. If using the agent feels like work, adoption slows. If it feels effortless, adoption accelerates and with it, scale. Effortlessness is not just about interface design; it encompasses the entire experience stack: onboarding, integration, responsiveness, training, and support. Leaders should treat "effortless execution" as a product principle from day one. This means designing agents and workflows so that the path from first use to measurable impact is as short and frictionless as possible. In parallel, it means selling a vision internally and demonstrating, through pilots, stories, and executive theater, that the agent is not just powerful but also unburdens the user.

Why It Matters to Corporations: Behavioral science proves that people overvalue ease. When an agent is positioned as something that removes work rather than adds to it, adoption increases, friction drops, and skepticism fades. Sell relief, not AI. What people want is not smarter, it is easier. Effortlessness is a competitive moat. In markets where many tools offer similar capabilities, the one that requires the least from the user wins, and wins faster by:

- **Accelerating Adoption Curves:** Lowering perceived effort increases the likelihood of behavior change.
- **Boosting Political Capital:** Leaders who champion "effortless" wins gain faster support from peers.
- **Improving Workforce Morale:** Employees associate the agent with relief rather than disruption.
- **Strengthening Business Case for Scale:** Positive user sentiment becomes evidence for further investment.
- **Increasing Competitive Agility:** Fast adoption enables quicker responses to market shifts.

Real-World Example: A Fortune 500 retailer launched a replenishment optimization agent to help store managers. To ensure a seamless experience, the rollout team designed the tool to auto-populate order forms, integrate smoothly with existing dashboards, and require no manual data entry. They also organized an "effortless challenge," which asked managers to track how much time the new process saved compared to the old one. This approach led 96% of managers to voluntarily adopt the tool within 30 days and become active advocates for broader implementation. By emphasizing ease of use, the initiative shifted from an ordinary IT rollout to a grassroots movement. In the race for corporate adoption, perceived effort matters just as much as actual performance. When you build and communicate for effortlessness, your agent will not only be accepted but eagerly sought after.

Principle 18: Reveal Hidden ROI$_2$

Definition: Use agent data to surface latent problems and drive actionable insights.

Return on intelligence (ROI$_2$) is the measurable value an agent creates when insight itself becomes an accretive asset.

Return on intelligence (ROI$_2$) is the measurable value an agent creates when insight itself becomes an accretive asset. The actual value of an AI agent is not just in the tasks it automates, but also in the intelligence it compounds. Its real power comes from the patterns it detects, patterns that human eyes often overlook or that remain buried beneath years of operational noise. By systematically gathering, analyzing, and sharing these insights, an agent begins to generate what can only be described as ROI$_2$. Through this return, the enterprise gains two powerful drivers of change: 1) hidden inefficiencies that quietly erode margins and 2) untapped opportunities that can generate new sources of growth. Leaders should therefore view agents not merely as doers but as discoverers and architects of continuous learning loops. Each output should be treated as a diagnostic lens on the enterprise's performance architecture. Every recommendation, variance flag, or anomaly should be evaluated not only for its immediate utility but also for the intelligence dividend it contributes to a deeper understanding of structural health, risk posture, and latent profitability, which defines a true ROI_2.

Why It Matters to Corporations: AI agents do more than execute; they observe. Their observations can uncover inefficiencies, bottlenecks, and missed revenue opportunities. When leveraged effectively, this intelligence becomes a valuable tool for funding future innovations. Your agent is not just a worker; it is a source of economic insights that can:

- **Transform Agents Into Strategic Advisors:** Moves the agent's role from operational support to profit generation.
- **Justify Further Investment:** Tangible discovery of hidden ROI_2 supports expanding agent capabilities.
- **Inform C-Suite Decisions:** Insights from real-world data improve capital allocation and strategic planning.
- **Build Enterprise Resilience:** Early detection of issues prevents revenue leakage and reputational damage.
- **Drive Continuous Improvement:** Insights feed a loop of targeted process redesign.

In large enterprises, a 1% efficiency gain can mean millions in recovered margin. Agents that reveal hidden ROI_2 provide leaders with a steady flow of these benefits, often in areas where nobody expected to find them.

Real-World Example: A global insurance company deployed a claims triage agent to speed up case routing. During this process, the agent's anomaly detection model found a group of claims that consistently took 40% longer to resolve, mainly due to gaps in initial documentation. This insight led to a simple change to intake forms, resulting in a 17% reduction in overall resolution time. The financial benefit came not just from automating the process but also from identifying and removing the bottleneck. The adjustment freed millions in working capital and boosted customer satisfaction scores, strengthening the brand's competitive edge. When you train agents to look beyond immediate outputs, they uncover structural inefficiencies, spot emerging opportunities, and provide leadership with actionable insights. In doing so, they don't just deliver ROI_2; they reveal it.

Principle 19: Prove the Return

Definition: Every agent needs an economic justification.

An AI agent without a clear economic justification is an expense searching for a purpose. In corporate settings, where resources are limited and competition for capital is fierce, every deployed agent must have an explicit, measurable reason for existence that appeals to both operational leaders and financial decision-makers. Every AI dollar should trace back to at least one of three ROI drivers: revenue expansion, operational efficiency, and/or risk reduction. Economic justification

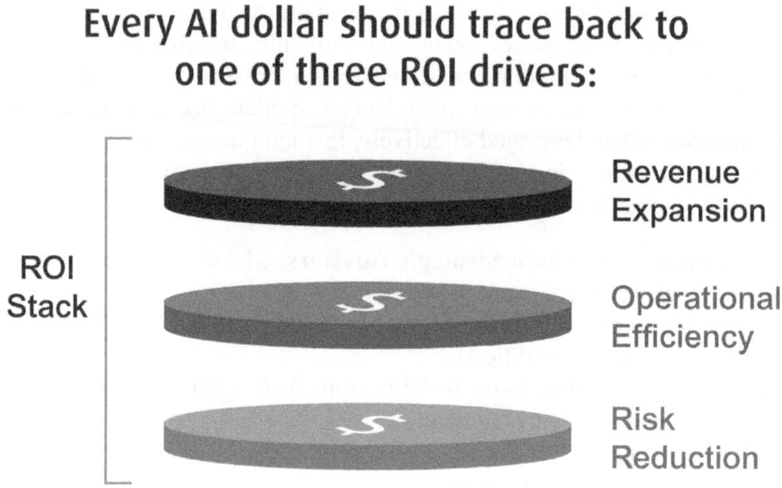

Figure 3.1 ROI stack showing three ROI drivers. Diagram by BMO Financial Group.

goes beyond just a cost-benefit calculation; it is a story supported by complex data. It explains how the agent will help achieve measurable business results, such as lowering operational costs, speeding up revenue generation, boosting productivity, or enhancing decision-making. The justification must be compelling enough to survive the scrutiny of CFOs, risk committees, and transformation boards. Without this anchor, agents risk falling into the category of "innovation curiosities" piloted, praised in early internal communications, and then quietly shelved when budgets tighten. This principle ensures that every agent's role is directly tied to creating enterprise value, making its continuation not just desirable but necessary.

Why It Matters to Corporations: Executives do not back ideas; they back returns. This principle ensures that every agent introduced into an enterprise has a clear, defensible, and recurring economic rationale, framed in language the CFO understands. You are not building AI; you are building a line item. Show the return or lose the agent. In a corporate setting, technology initiatives succeed when they survive the triple test of viability (can it work reliably at scale?), desirability (will the end users adopt it?), and profitability (does it improve the economics of the business?). Economic justification operates as the third and most decisive pillar. Here is why it matters:

- **Boardroom Resilience:** Initiatives tied to specific economic metrics are more complex to cut. When transformation priorities shift, those with measurable ROI keep their funding.

- **Capital Allocation Discipline:** In large organizations, projects compete for budget. An agent that can show it reduces cost-to-serve by 15%, accelerates onboarding times by 30%, or enables $50M in incremental revenue stands out in budget discussions.
- **Cultural Credibility:** Agents framed as economic assets command more respect from line managers and frontline teams. They're seen not as experimental overhead, but as revenue or efficiency drivers.
- **Strategic Portfolio Management:** Linking agents to economic KPIs allows the enterprise to compare them objectively, prioritize the highest performers, and quickly retire underperformers.

By embedding economic justification from day one, you not only protect the project from premature termination but also create a standard for scale. Once the financial model is validated, you have the foundation to expand into other domains with credibility and speed.

Real-World Example: A multinational bank developed a highly advanced fraud-detection agent, but it couldn't be deployed. When reframed in terms of reducing false positives (and the number of call center hours saved), it gained immediate executive approval. The agent did not change. The math did. A central retail bank piloted a customer service agent designed to handle credit card disputes. The pilot team focused on speed-to-market and user satisfaction, neglecting to quantify its financial impact. The agent worked well, resolving cases faster than human staff, but without an economic framework in place, the value remained anecdotal. Contrast this with a competing bank that launched a similar agent but linked it directly to economic KPIs: reducing case handling time from 22 minutes to 7 minutes, decreasing dispute resolution costs by $4.80 per case, and increasing retention rates among high-value customers by 3%. These metrics resulted in $12 million in annualized savings and $8 million in preserved customer lifetime value. When budget season arrived, the first bank's project was reduced in scope, as it was seen as a "nice to have." The second bank not only expanded its agents' remit but also secured funding to develop two more specialized agents in adjacent areas.

Agents are not immune to corporate survival pressures. Those who cannot prove their worth in financial terms are the first to be deprioritized. When you require an economic justification for every agent, you:

- **Ensure Strategic Alignment:** Agents are built to serve business outcomes, not tech experimentation.
- **Safeguard Budget:** A clear financial case protects funding through leadership changes and budget cycles.
- **Accelerate Adoption:** Business units embrace agents that make measurable contributions to their P&L.

This principle also reinforces cultural discipline: it signals to the organization that AI is not a playground, but a performance asset. The competitive reality is apparent: the companies winning with AI are those that integrate financial thinking into technical design from day one. They don't just measure value after launch; they build for value before the first line of code is written. If an agent's economic case is unclear, it should be paused, redesigned, or retired. Anything else is a silent drain on the organization's resources.

Principle 20: Govern the Future

Definition: The human-to-agent ratio is not just a number; it is a corporate truth serum.

The Human:Agent ratio measures the total human labor force, including full-time employees, offshore staff, and contractors, relative to the enterprise-grade AI agents deployed in live production workflows. The ratio reveals, without the noise of narrative or spin, the extent to which AI agents have been woven into the fabric of your enterprise workforce. A declining ratio signals operational maturity in the AI era: the shift from human-exclusive workflows toward orchestrated, AI-assisted operations that can scale without proportionate cost increases. To "govern the ratio" is to manage the transformation of your enterprise. It involves making this metric central to strategic decisions, serving as a test to determine if your AI strategy is more than just a presentation slide. It reflects not only technology adoption but also cultural integration, operational discipline, and leadership courage. Boardrooms are full of vanity metrics – numbers that sound impressive but are disconnected from operational reality. Injecting thousands of useless agents that do not drive the principles in this book to manipulate the ratio is plausible gamification, which is why the ratio's definition clearly specifies the agents are quality, enterprise-grade and in production workflows. In the AI transformation era, the Human:Agent ratio stands out as stubbornly, refreshingly unglamorous. It has no emotional halo, no marketing gloss. It tells you, in precise mathematical terms, whether your organization is structurally integrating AI agents or simply experimenting. The power of this ratio lies in its objectivity.

A bank may trumpet AI chatbots, algorithmic credit scoring, or "centers of excellence." Still, if the ratio remains at 100:1, meaning one enterprise AI agent for every hundred human workers, it is in the emerging stage. That is not transformation; it is tinkering. Leaders who govern this ratio understand that transformation is not achieved by showcasing AI pilots but by embedding AI into the bloodstream of operations. Every movement in the ratio, downward toward full orchestration, should be intentional, tied to a business case, and rigorously measured. This is where behavioral science comes into play. Humans respond

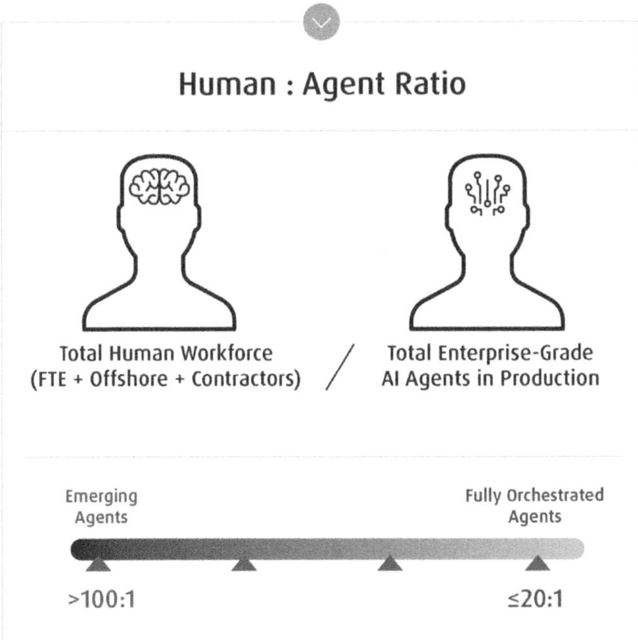

Figure 3.2 Human:Agent ratio and implications for organizations. Diagram by BMO Financial Group.

to clarity and social proof. When leaders can point to complex data showing the Human:Agent ratio shifting, backed by real-world outcomes in productivity, margin expansion, or client experience, they create belief. And belief drives adoption, both internally and in the market. In competitive terms, your ratio also serves as a scarcity signal. There are only so many quarters you have before competitors close the gap. Moving from 100:1 to 20:1 is not merely an efficiency play; it is an existential positioning move. In the AI era, the companies that govern the ratio will govern their future. In any large-scale AI transformation, the Human:Agent ratio should be regarded as a KPI alongside revenue, margin, and efficiency metrics. It provides the most direct quantitative indicator of AI adoption and how well operations are integrated. The Human:Agent ratio (H:A) is as follows:

$$(H:A) = \frac{Total\ Human\ Workforce\ (FTE + offshores + Contractors)}{Total\ Enterprise\ Grade\ AI\ Agents\ in\ Production} \tag{3.1}$$

Enterprise-grade AI agents are defined as those that:

- Operate within live production workflows.
- Meet security, compliance, and scalability standards.
- Are embedded into repeatable business processes with measurable outputs.

A lower ratio implies **higher agent leverage**, meaning more digital capacity per human. A higher ratio suggests **lower automation leverage** and more human-intensive operations. The ratio offers leaders:

- **Visibility:** It strips away narrative bias and reveals the structural truth of AI penetration.
- **Comparability:** It allows benchmarking over time and against peers.
- **Discipline:** It forces alignment between AI strategy and actual execution.

By governing the ratio, leadership commits to tracking, influencing, and accelerating the integration of AI agents, not as isolated experiments but as scaled, orchestrated contributors to enterprise value creation.

Why It Matters to Corporations: Corporations exist to generate value: financial, strategic, and reputational. In the era of technological transformation, the value equation changes: operational leverage is no longer driven purely by human headcount productivity but by the partnership between human and digital labor. A corporation with a high Human:Agent ratio relies heavily on human execution, which is expensive, slow to grow, and challenging to adapt during market pressures. A lower ratio, achieved smartly, creates a more flexible, efficient, and resilient operating model. From a financial standpoint, this ratio directly impacts profit margins. AI agents, once implemented, incur minimal additional costs per transaction or task. Agents can be expanded without needing proportional increases in salaries, benefits, or physical infrastructure. This is operational leverage at its purest. From a risk perspective, the ratio signals resilience. A high level of AI orchestration can help companies manage workforce disruptions caused by economic downturns, regulatory shocks, or supply chain issues without significantly reducing productivity. The ratio serves as an early indicator of market agility, with corporations with lower ratios better equipped to implement innovations, modify processes, and respond to client needs more rapidly than their competitors. Insights from behavioral science indicate that visible, measurable progress is a vital factor driving organizational change.

Leaders can reinforce the tangible impact of AI integration by presenting ratio changes together with operational results. For example, noting, "our shift from 80:1 to 60:1 enabled us to cut loan underwriting times by 40%." This makes it clear that AI is bringing measurable transformation now, not just offering a distant future goal. The ratio also creates a sense of urgency, highlighting that each quarter of delay is an opportunity for rivals to close the gap or overtake you. Once a market leader falls behind in orchestrating AI, catching up becomes exponentially more resource and culture intensive. Finally, the ratio helps unite the executive team; differing opinions about AI's promise or risk are set aside when everyone understands a straightforward ratio. In the boardroom, it's a number that equally calls for justification or improvement.

Real-World Example: At a North American financial institution, the Human:Agent ratio began as an internal transformational KPI. They started at a clear "emerging" stage, with an estimated >100:1. AI agents existed, but they were mostly in pilots, proofs of concept, or narrow use cases like call center triage. In Year 1 of their transformation roadmap, they deployed enterprise-grade AI agents into high-volume, rules-based workflows. These included transaction monitoring, retail onboarding document verification, and specific fraud detection tasks. They closed the year at ~75:1. In Year 2, they expanded AI orchestration across cross-functional processes, including loan underwriting, treasury operations, and multi-channel customer support. They also integrated AI into internal decision-support systems, enabling analysts to process complex datasets in hours rather than days. This drove the ratio toward ~40:1. By Year 3, the target is ≤20:1, classified as *fully orchestrated.* At that stage, AI agents will handle first-pass decision-making in standard cases across the enterprise, with humans focusing on exceptions, innovation, and client relationship management. The result is not just cost optimization, it is strategic capacity creation. Moving from 100:1 to 20:1 frees thousands of human hours, which they redeploy into higher-margin client activities. And because this movement is measured, it sustains organizational momentum and stakeholder confidence.

Starting with the (H:A) ratio is a critical first step in measuring accountability that agents are built to drive business value outcomes. However, to make a real impact on the balance sheet, institutions and CFOs will need to modify classical operating leverage calculations to an evolved measure, **intelligent operating leverage (IOL)**. In classical corporate finance, **operating leverage (OL)** measures how a change in revenue translates into a change in operating income (EBIT). The higher the OL, the more sensitive profits are to revenue growth; a slight increase in revenue yields a magnified increase in profit, due to fixed-cost absorption. In an AI-augmented enterprise, the boundary between fixed and variable costs shifts dramatically. AI agents behave economically like quasi-fixed assets: they scale at a near-zero marginal cost once deployed. Meanwhile, human capital (and the ratio between humans and agents) becomes the true driver of scalable productivity, rather than headcount alone. Thus, we evolve the equation to intelligent operating leverage, which measures the incremental output or operating efficiency achieved per unit change in the Human:Agent mix.

$$IOL = OL \times f(H:A) \tag{3.2}$$

Where:

- $f(H:A)$ represents the **agent leverage multiplier,** the productivity elasticity created by AI augmentation.

We define $f(H:A)$ as:

$$f(H:A) = \left(\frac{A}{H+A}\right)^{\beta} \tag{3.3}$$

Where:

- $\frac{A}{H+A}$ expresses **the proportion of digital labor** in total productive capacity
- β is an elasticity coefficient capturing **how much agent adoption influences operating efficiency** (estimated empirically by measuring how marginal cost declines as agent ratio increases).

IOL preserves the traditional leverage effect, and the agent leverage multiplier amplifies or dampens it depending on adoption maturity. When agents account for a larger share of total productive work, marginal cost declines, increasing leverage. To expose where AI affects leverage, one can further decompose EBIT into cost structure components:

$$IOL = \frac{(Revenue - Variable\ Costs\ (H:A))}{(Revenue - Variable\ Costs\ (H:A) - Fixed\ Costs)} \times \left(\frac{A}{H+A}\right)^{\beta} \tag{3.4}$$

Where:

- $Variable\ Costs\ (H:A)$ reflect the declining marginal cost curve as agents scale, effectively modeling the hybrid workforce as an elastic production frontier.

When $H:A$ **decreases** (i.e., more agents per human), **operating leverage increases,** but only if the incremental agents sustain quality and customer outcomes.

- When $\beta \rightarrow 1$, agent productivity scales linearly (each additional agent produces proportional efficiency).
- When $\beta > 1$, the enterprise enters *superlinear scalability*: compounding efficiency, typical of fully digitized workflows.
- When $\beta < 1$, diminishing returns set in, signaling over-automation or friction between human and digital labor.

The **intelligent operating leverage model** reframes how enterprises measure scale in the age of AI agents. At its center is the **Human:Agent ratio**, the new productivity denominator that balances digital capacity with human judgment. Surrounding it are six drivers of enterprise value:

1. Revenue expansion (growth through intelligent scaling).
2. Cost efficiency (automation-driven margin improvement).
3. Risk optimization (proactive, data-led mitigation).
4. Experience differentiation (customer and employee experience).
5. Trust & transparency (ethical, explainable deployment).
6. Intelligent operating leverage (compounding value from human–agent balance).

Together, they illustrate that sustainable advantage does not come from cost control alone, but from the intelligent orchestration of human and artificial capabilities. When the ratio is governed well, every spoke of the model strengthens simultaneously: revenue grows, costs compress, risk reduces, experience improves, and trust compounds. The intelligent operating leverage model is the new architecture of *Return on Intelligence*: a system where empathy and economics converge to create measurable, intelligent enterprise performance.

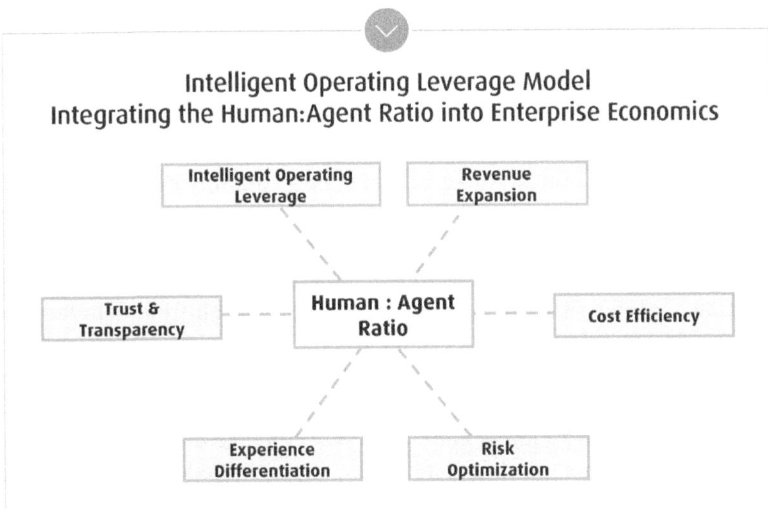

Figure 3.3 Intelligent operating leverage model – integrating the Human:Agent ratio into enterprise economics. Diagram by Kristin Milchanowski and Isabel Schaad.

*The **intelligent operating leverage model** is the new architecture of Return on Intelligence: a system where empathy and economics converge to create measurable, intelligent enterprise performance.*

In traditional finance, operating leverage was defined by how much fixed infrastructure you carried. In intelligent enterprises, it is determined by how well you balance human judgment with agent capacity. The Human:Agent ratio is the new denominator of leverage. IOL is the measure that tells leaders not how much they can automate, but how intelligently they can scale. The enterprise that governs this ratio well doesn't just improve margins, it compounds intelligence. The Human:Agent ratio forces discipline. It is not a mood, a belief, or a slogan; it is a measurable indicator of how effectively an enterprise is reshaping its operating model for the AI age.

Principle 21: Mirror, Not Mask

Definition: Use agent dashboards to reflect reality without bias.

In regulated sectors, AI dashboards must reflect reality precisely as it is, without "smoothing" for optics. An agent that masks volatility or risk for the sake of presentation undermines trust and exposes leadership to compliance breaches. "Mirror, Not Mask" is both a technical and political principle. In the enterprise world, AI agents are not "set and forget" assets; they are dynamic entities that live inside evolving processes, market pressures, and shifting data landscapes. Organizations should treat agents as living systems that are continuously audited for accuracy, fairness, compliance, and performance and improved with the same frequency and urgency. Relentless auditing means more than a quarterly check-in. It requires automated performance dashboards, bias scans, failure mode detection, and user feedback loops embedded into daily operations. It is an intentional, ongoing process that identifies drift before it becomes costly, catches compliance issues before they escalate, and validates that the agent is still aligned with the business objectives it was created to serve. Improvement is not optional; it is the twin obligation of audit. Once insights are captured, they must be acted upon quickly, whether that means retraining models, adjusting workflows, or re-engineering the agent entirely. This principle elevates governance from merely following rules to gaining a competitive edge: those who audit and improve more quickly can out-innovate slower rivals while reducing risks.

Why It Matters to Corporations: Dashboards are more than just summaries; they are reflections of reality. When agents present precisely what is happening without spin, they become trusted sources of truth. Transparency builds legitimacy. Honesty improves usefulness. An agent who tells the truth is more valuable than one who performs well but hides the facts. Trust starts with transparency. Accurate, open reporting enhances resilience against crisis narratives. Politically, providing unvarnished data positions the executive sponsor as credible and accountable, key qualities in regulatory hearings and public disclosures. Behavioral science warns that once trust is lost, it becomes much harder to rebuild. In boardroom discussions, credibility is currency. An agent who consistently reflects operational truth, even when it is uncomfortable, safeguards the long-term relationship among management, regulators, and investors. Continuous audit and improvement are not overhead; they are the operational discipline that distinguishes organizations with a sustainable AI advantage from those whose agents quietly slip into irrelevance or liability as it:

- **Prevents Silent Failures:** AI agents can degrade subtly over time due to data drift, changing user behavior, or external shifts in the market or regulatory landscape. Without ongoing audits, these degradations go unnoticed until they cause visible damage, customer loss, reputational harm, or regulatory penalties.
- **Supports Regulatory Readiness:** In financial services, health care, and other regulated sectors, demonstrating continuous oversight is no longer optional. Regulators will expect auditable logs, model performance histories, and evidence of corrective action.
- **Protects ROI:** The economic case for an agent depends on its sustained performance. Without relentless improvement, ROI erodes quickly. Regular performance tuning protects and extends that return.
- **Accelerates Learning Across the Portfolio:** Audit insights from one agent can be applied to others, creating a cross-agent learning network. This reduces time-to-correction and accelerates organizational AI maturity.
- **Enhances Trust Across Stakeholders:** Leadership, frontline teams, and customers alike gain confidence in agents when they see a pattern of measured, transparent, and acted-upon improvement.

Real-World Example: Energy utilities manage high-stakes infrastructure under constant regulatory and public scrutiny. A European utility's AI load-balancing agent displayed unadjusted real-time grid stress data during a heatwave. Instead of masking peaks to avoid public concern, transparency enabled proactive investment in demand-response measures. The result: no blackouts, a strengthened regulator relationship, and a board that approved expanded AI integration. In utilities and other regulated sectors, masking data for short-term optics is a long-term liability. A dashboard that "mirrors" reality is an act of political self-preservation and strategic trust-building, beyond only a technical design choice.

Organizations should treat agent oversight as an always-on capability by integrating continuous auditing and improvement into their operational culture. Oversight ensures agents stay aligned with business goals, provide consistent ROI, and uphold stakeholder trust by lowering risk through early detection of performance issues or compliance problems. Other benefits include:

- Increased agent lifetime value via ongoing performance enhancements,
- Accelerated organizational learning through cross-agent knowledge sharing, and
- Greater stakeholder confidence through visible accountability and responsiveness.

Relentless auditing and improvement create a cultural expectation: if an agent operates in your enterprise, it will be measured, optimized, and kept fit for purpose at all times. Anything less is a disservice to both your balance sheet and your brand. The enterprise leaders who commit to this discipline will not just maintain competitive advantage; they will compound it. Those who do not will eventually find themselves relying on agents that are not just underperforming but actively undermining their business objectives.

Chapter 3 Conclusion

Economic arguments always trump innovative language. When agents prove their value in terms that executives already understand—money, risk, and time—agents transcend trends and become mission infrastructure. Show the numbers. Frame the relief. Reveal the gold. In the final analysis, data without justification is noise; economics without evidence is speculation. Throughout this chapter, we have observed that in the enterprise arena, whether in banking boardrooms, healthcare networks, energy utilities, or retail command centers, the political, financial, and operational survival of an AI agent depends on its ability to demonstrate its value while acting as an unwavering steward of truth. Automating a broken process is the fastest way to scale dysfunction. By fixing before automating, we not only reduce operational risk but also protect the sponsor's political capital. Data trails, if mishandled, can destroy adoption and invite scrutiny; the agent must be both a source of truth and a shield. Anchor the agent's legitimacy in radical transparency because masking reality is not a design choice, but a governance failure. The thread binding these principles is the principle that value must be self-evident, continuous, and defensible. Initial ROI projections are not enough. The agent must feed its business case through ongoing metrics: avoided costs, captured revenue, risk mitigation, and workforce efficiency gains. In practice, this means every AI program requires a dual operating rhythm: one focused on delivering outcomes, the other on narrating those outcomes to decision-makers. The CFO must see the quantified value; the CRO must know the risk reduction; the COO must see the operational gains. Without this ongoing justification loop, even high-performing agents become expendable when the strategic winds shift. In board governance terms, the six principles of this chapter intersect with four critical KPIs as shown in Figure 3.4.

Figure 3.4 Four critical KPIs intersecting with six principles for boards to consider. Diagram by BMO Financial Group.

Key Takeaways

- Agent economics are not static. They compound when data is leveraged to justify expansion.
- Every agent decision must be grounded in ROI that leadership can defend and the market can recognize.
- Ratio governance is the balance of human-to-agent contribution used as a strategic lever.

- Without evidence, adoption risks becoming theater; without theater, momentum dies.
- Industry leaders convert ratio gains into public proof points that draw capital, talent, and market trust.

The Human:Agent ratio reveals, without the noise of narrative or spin, the extent to which AI agents have been woven into the fabric of your enterprise workforce. In the AI era, governance of this ratio is the scoreboard of your strategic relevance. Lead it or be led by those who do. The principles in Chapter 3 establish the foundation of an AI enterprise that gains both internal and external legitimacy. However, these principles are only as practical as the governance structure that supports them. The time to act is now.

- **Set the Target:** Define the Human:Agent ratio that aligns with your strategic ambitions.
- **Measure Relentlessly:** Make it a standing agenda item in executive reviews.
- **Link to Outcomes:** Show in clear, financial terms how ratio gains translate into market advantage.
- **Broadcast Success:** Turn each milestone into social proof that attracts talent, customers, and capital.

The synthesis of these metrics provides the kind of full-spectrum justification that resonates with a modern board: financially rigorous, politically astute, and operationally credible. Every AI agent must be engineered for political safety, not just technical performance. In most large organizations, the failure of a single AI initiative not only renders the technology obsolete but can also stall the entire AI program for years. This occurs when political safety is ignored, even if objectively successful agents risk being retired for optics or reputational risk management. Political safety is achieved by:

- Avoiding the scaling of flawed processes.
- Ensuring data outputs can withstand scrutiny.
- Designing interfaces that executives can personally navigate without handholding.
- Producing value beyond the original scope.
- Quantifying returns in CFO-grade language.
- Displaying performance data without manipulation.

Persona Highlights

Jordan, Chief Strategy & Transformation Officer

- Anchors on Human:Agent ratio as the new transformation metric to "Govern the Future."

- *Key takeaway:* Ratios connect adoption to shareholder narratives, making strategy measurable.

Claire, Chief Financial Officer

- Resonates with "Prove the Return" and "Fix First, Then Automate."
- *Key takeaway:* Every agent must prove ROI with disciplined, auditable business cases.

Rafael, Chief Technology Officer

- Views "Reveal Hidden ROI_2" as a means to elevate technology from a cost center to a profit enabler.
- *Key takeaway:* Agents should surface inefficiencies in workflows that technology alone could not expose.

Simone, Chief Human Resources Officer

- Focuses on "Effortless Is Everything" and the Human:Agent ratio.
- *Key takeaway:* Agents that deliver effortless experiences reduce burnout and rebalance work, improving morale.

Mo, Chief Marketing Officer

- Values "Mirror, Not Mask" for brand trust and "Effortless Is Everything" for customer engagement.
- *Key takeaway:* Agents that deliver frictionless experiences and transparent metrics reinforce both brand promise and customer loyalty.

Part I Conclusion

AI agents must live inside the same accountability frameworks as any other capital asset. They must have measurable ROI, defensible assumptions, and transparent economics. When you can explain your Human:Agent ratio to your CFO, justify deployment to your regulator, and connect output to enterprise value, you've crossed from promise to proof. Return on intelligence begins here: when every agent deployed has an owner, a metric, and a P&L reason to exist. The blueprints are drawn. The math works. The architecture of AI is solid. But technology doesn't scale through logic; it scales through leadership. The next phase is not about models or metrics; it's about belief. How do you create momentum in an environment built on skepticism and politics? How do you manage perception without losing control? Part II shifts focus from how agents work to how organizations change, where leadership becomes choreography, adoption becomes theater, and every visible win becomes a political asset.

DOI: 10.4324/9781003749899-6

Part II

Influence

Leadership, Culture, and Organizational Transformation

AI may be engineered in code, but it is adopted in culture. In this part, we enter the leadership domain, the power structures, incentives, and narratives that determine whether an agent thrives or dies. Part II explores how to secure executive sponsorship, build trust with functional leaders, and stage early wins that create organizational "air cover" (Chapter 4). Agents are not neutral; they are political actors in enterprise life. Success depends as much on emotional intelligence as on technical intelligence. Once sponsorship and belief are secured, we turn to adaptability, transforming the organization from static to self-learning (Chapter 5). Culture becomes an operating system, not a slogan.

DOI: 10.4324/9781003749899-7

Chapter 4

Leadership, Influence, and Political Buy-In

AI agents are not merely technical deployments; they represent acts of organizational persuasion. Without executive support, political alignment, and frontline advocacy, even the most advanced AI systems can stall. Chapter 4 introduces the influence blueprint: principles for building alliances, crafting strategic narratives, and positioning AI agents as essential to business growth. This is not about coding; it is about controlling the organizational chessboard. Each principle is rooted in behavioral science, such as authority framing, social proof, and emotional resonance, to move stakeholders from skeptics to supporters.

Strategy falters when influence is ignored. In every large enterprise, the path from a strong idea to a funded, scaled reality passes through people who grant permission, allocate capital, carry risk, and live with the consequences. AI agents, no matter how capable, succeed only when they elevate leaders, reduce political friction, and generate wins others are proud to claim. This chapter translates that truth into practice. The principles collected here are not about algorithms; they are about authority, status, and the careful choreography of credit. The central premise is straightforward: leaders adopt what preserves their standing, teams support what advances their goals, and organizations scale what feels unescapable. Agents that compete with leaders, steal the spotlight, or arrive without a sponsor do not last. Agents that make leaders faster, safer, and visibly effective become non-negotiable. That is why this chapter concentrates on narrative, optics, and sequencing as much as on performance. We will map the power before we design, align the agent to the leadership agenda, stage wins as executive theater, and win the gatekeepers and the frontline in the order that lowers resistance and compounds momentum.

Principle 22: Agents Lift Leaders

Definition: Agents make leaders look good.

AI agents should never overshadow the human leaders they serve; their highest purpose is to elevate those leaders. This means removing friction, handling

DOI: 10.4324/9781003749899-8

the heavy lifting, and delivering results that position leaders to make faster, sharper, and more strategic decisions. In the same way, a world-class chief of staff anticipates needs, synthesizes information, and ensures flawless execution. At the same time, the executive receives recognition, while an AI agent operates in the background to enhance leadership authority. This is not about minimizing the agent's capability. It is about positioning the agent's outputs as the leader's achievements. The more the agent streamlines complexity and shields leaders from operational drag, the more leadership can focus on strategy, influence, and growth. At the same time, leaders must be willing to stand in the spotlight while acknowledging the infrastructure, human and machine, that makes their success possible. When agents handle the burdens of scale, volume, and velocity, leaders gain the bandwidth to shape the organization's trajectory.

Why It Matters to Corporations: This creates a strong model for sustainable adoption. Corporations operate in an environment where perception is closely linked to performance. Leaders are judged not only by results but also by their ability to inspire trust, manage political capital, and deliver consistently. In practice, this means:

- **Operational Shielding:** Allow the agent to handle operational tasks that would otherwise drain leadership resources quietly.
- **Political Cover:** Safeguard the leader's political standing by ensuring results are attributed in ways that strengthen their influence.
- **Cultural Alignment:** Promote the idea that agents exist to serve leadership and teams, not to replace them.

This dual approach not only speeds up adoption but also ensures that agents are integrated into the organization's leadership fabric. It's much easier to expand and scale technology when it is perceived as supporting leadership rather than competing with it.

Real-World Example: A global investment bank introduced an AI agent to oversee real-time risk exposure across multiple trading desks. This agent can analyze billions of data points in milliseconds, detect anomalies, and suggest mitigation strategies. Rather than spotlighting the AI, bank leadership cast it as "the advisor's advisor." Risk officers received alerts and recommendations from the agent, synthesized them, and briefed senior executives. Leadership publicly credited a new "enhanced risk management framework" with improving capital efficiency and reducing exposure by 14%, while internally recognizing the AI agent's critical role. By allowing human leaders to present the results while the agent handled the analytical work, the bank maintained political harmony, avoided cultural resistance, and positioned the AI as a force multiplier rather than a rival. Within a year, this approach extended to credit, compliance, and portfolio management.

An AI agent that uplifts leadership while remaining discreet delivers strategic and political value. In enterprise AI adoption, longevity hinges on aligning technology's abilities with leadership authority. When agents empower leaders and contribute to their success, the technology's survival becomes intertwined with the leader's continued influence. By appreciating AI agents as trusted partners, leaders create a culture where AI is seen as an enabler rather than a threat. The result is a virtuous cycle:

1. Leaders advocate for the technology because it boosts their performance.
2. Teams embrace the technology because it supports, not threatens, their leaders.
3. The organization expands the technology because it is both politically safe and strategically essential.

In corporate power dynamics, such alignment is imperative; it determines whether an initiative remains a stalled pilot or evolves into a mission-critical system embedded in the enterprise's DNA.

Principle 23: Make It Serve, Not Steer

Definition: Make the agent serve leadership's agenda, not its own.

An AI agent's credibility in an enterprise depends on how well it aligns with leadership's goals. The idea that a technology is *steering* strategy rather than *serving* it can lead to resistance, especially among executives who see their decision-making authority as a source of legitimacy and power. The role of an AI agent is to enhance leadership's capabilities, provide insights, automate tasks, and clarify issues, while ensuring that humans retain the final decision-making authority.

Why It Matters to Corporations: Corporate leaders are gatekeepers of influence. If they feel undermined or bypassed by a technology, they will block it, regardless of its objective value. This is especially true in organizations with strong founder cultures, deeply established hierarchies, or regulated environments where accountability is inseparable from decision-making authority. Positioning an AI agent as a "servant" to leadership does not diminish its power; it boosts adoption by lowering political risk. Behavioral science explains this through the principle of "ego preservation." People are more likely to accept tools that make them look better without threatening their status.

Real-World Example: A multinational manufacturing company implemented a supply chain optimization agent that initially provided direct procurement recommendations to category managers. While accurate, these suggestions bypassed managers' evaluation processes, leading to quiet resistance and low adoption. The approach was then redesigned to frame the agent as a "decision support partner." Instead of issuing commands, it offered ranked options with trade-offs and clearly stated, "final selection at manager's discretion." Adoption grew significantly. Category managers began referencing the agent's analysis in leadership meetings, and within a year, it was included in quarterly procurement strategy reviews. An AI agent's purpose is to enhance leadership's influence. The more leaders see the agent as "on their team," the faster it will be embraced and integrated into the organization's decision-making culture.

Principle 24: Essential, Not Extra

Definition: Build a narrative that makes agents mission-critical.

An AI agent should never be perceived as a luxury feature or an experimental add-on. An agent must be positioned as an indispensable part of the enterprise operating system. This means the agent isn't simply helpful; it is vital. Critical processes, decision-making flows, and leadership priorities should visibly rely on its capabilities. Internal perception matters as much as performance. The winning strategy is to connect the agent directly to leadership's clearly stated objectives, provide undeniable proof points early on, and make it evident that removing the agent would set the business back. By combining operational necessity with a carefully crafted origin story portraying the agent as the natural next step in the company's growth, you reinforce its position. It is no longer just an optional tool; it is now part of the company's identity. An agent's technical capabilities must align with the workflows that define the company's value, and its narrative must be rooted in leadership's vision for the future.

Why It Matters to Corporations: In large organizations, political capital is just as significant as financial capital when introducing new technologies. An agent perceived as "extra" is easy to cut during budget cuts or leadership changes. However, an agent is seen as vital, integrated into the business, and able to withstand reorganizations, budget reviews, and leadership shifts. To position an agent as essential, two key actions are necessary: 1) embed it into workflows and 2) shape the narrative early. The agent must be incorporated into the processes that drive value, compliance, or competitive edge. If it can be bypassed with ease, it is not essential. From the start, its introduction should be accompanied by a story directly linked to the organization's mission and the CEO's priorities. "Build a Narrative That Makes Agents Mission-Critical" is not just a side note here; it is central to shaping the narrative early. The story should be repeated, reinforced, and echoed by influential stakeholders so that adoption aligns with the company's vision, not just as a tactical upgrade. The best narratives are forward-looking. They don't just sell the current feature set; they frame the agent as the bridge to a more competitive, efficient, or innovative future. In this way, both the agent's operational and symbolic roles combine to create an unshakable perception of necessity.

Real-World Example: A multinational logistics company faced rising fuel costs, tighter delivery windows, and growing environmental compliance requirements. They developed an AI agent called "Atlas" to optimize fleet routing in real time. Atlas was not introduced as a generic routing tool. Instead, leadership positioned it as the company's strategic solution to the "last-mile profitability crisis" detailed in their annual report. Atlas was first deployed strategically in regions with the highest revenue, where delays and inefficiencies most impacted the bottom line. Within six months, Atlas cut average delivery times by 17% and reduced fuel use per delivery by 12%, saving millions in operating costs. But the key to Atlas's success wasn't just the numbers; it was the story. Every quarterly earnings call referenced Atlas as a "strategic capability," the CEO mentioned it in shareholder letters, and frontline managers were given talking points to remind teams that Atlas was the "profit engine in the driver's seat." By the time budgets were reviewed the following fiscal year, eliminating Atlas would have been seen internally as financial negligence.

When you merge operational necessity with a compelling origin story, you don't just secure adoption, you secure permanence. The agent becomes part of the company's identity, not just its toolkit.

- Without operational embedding, you have a great demo but no power base.
- Without a narrative, you have a silent workhorse that can be quietly replaced.
- With both, you have an irreplaceable, mission-critical capability that scales with the enterprise.

This is why, when considering your next AI agent deployment, you must ask not only "*What can it do?*" but "*What will the story be?*" The answer to the latter will determine whether your agent thrives or vanishes in the face of the winds of change.

Principle 25: Map the Power

Definition: Build stakeholder maps before agent design.

Pause and assess who genuinely influences the outcome, before writing a single prompt. In enterprises, the shortest distance between "we have a prototype" and "we are live at scale" is rarely a straight line. It bends around committees, crosses jurisdictions, and passes through careers. "Map the Power" converts that complexity into a tractable plan by identifying who can say yes, who can say no, and whose daily work will determine whether the tool is quietly ignored or actively used. A stakeholder map names sponsors, buyers, approvers, operators, skeptics, and swing voters. It records incentives, anxieties, and non-negotiables. It pairs each persona with a benefit (what they gain), a safeguard (what risk is contained), and a visible proof (the moment that will convince them). It also sequences engagement: whose endorsement must be public early, whose consent is private but essential, whose involvement should wait until the first proof exists. The output is not a mural; it is an operating document: a one-page grid that tells the build team when to invite Legal, when to pre-wire the union rep, when to brief the CFO, when to let the frontline test privately, and when to book the showcase. Build without it, and you will relearn the same political lessons at a high cost.

Why It Matters to Corporations: The power map is a risk register in disguise. Most "failed tech" stories are actually "failed alignment" stories. A head of compliance who feels bypassed, a financial planning and analysis (FP&A) lead who cannot tie metrics to the P&L, a frontline manager whose workload goes up in the name of progress, any one of them can slow you down by quarters. A map brings these hazards into the light early enough to design around them. As one CIO of a global 300 logistics firm noted, "Once we had the map, the conversations got shorter. People said yes faster because we arrived prepared." The benefits of doing so compound:

- **Shorter Approvals:** When Risk and Legal see their concerns addressed through measures like data minimization, audit trails, and reversibility, they move faster. Early drafts can incorporate their language, not just their signatures.
- **Cleaner Scoping:** If the frontline's tolerance for change is low this quarter (peak season, regulatory exam, merger), you can narrow the scope or shift the first deployment to a warmer site. Politics dictates sequence; sequence protects momentum.
- **Sponsorship Velocity:** When the sponsor knows which peers need to be convinced and what convinces them, they spend their capital efficiently. A five-minute proof clip to the COO beats a 50-page deck to a committee chair who cannot say yes.
- **Quiet Resistance Detection:** Mapping skeptics and swing voters surfaces the "no" that will not be said in the big room. You can design small tests and private demos to move them from "maybe not" to "let's see."

Use simple, durable patterns:

- **Benefit/Safeguard/Proof:** One sentence each per stakeholder. If you cannot write them, you are not ready for the meeting.
- **Order of Operations:** One row that shows the order in which you will ask, show, and escalate. The wrong meeting at the wrong time is a month lost.
- **Scarcity Wedge:** Limited early access for a few credible teams turns them into advocates and creates pull from others.

Real-World Example: A European insurer planned a claims triage agent. Early excitement masked the fundamental constraint: the national works council and a vigilant data-protection officer. The initial plan was to build, then "take them through it." Legal quietly advised against that path. The team paused to create the map. They identified the council chair's primary concern (surveillance creep), the data protection officer's (DPO) non-negotiables (purpose limitation, role-based access, redaction by default), and the frontline's fear (loss of discretion). They wrote one page that tied the agent's benefits ("faster resolution, fewer handoffs"), safeguards ("default aggregation, drill-down by exception, published access logs"), and proofs (a pilot cell with opt-in volunteers and a weekly joint dashboard review). They sequenced engagement: private demos for the chair and DPO, followed by a pilot at a single site with union observers, and finally an executive showcase with the pilot manager presenting. The result: consent with conditions on the first try, a 28% reduction in touch-time, and a smoother national rollout. "We were included, not surprised," the chair said on record. That quote, circulated internally, became social proof that unlocked the following program. Agents do not fail for lack of math; they fail for lack of maps. A power map is the cheapest insurance policy you can buy. To institutionalize it:

- **Make the map a gate.** No design sprint begins without a current stakeholder grid; no launch begins without an engagement log.
- **Keep it live.** Update after every meeting and record objections and how you addressed them. Good memory beats good intentions.
- **Put names to proofs.** Don't say "compliance sign-off." Say "Anita will sign if she sees X." Then build X.
- **Use scarcity ethically.** Offer early seats to those who commit to share data and lessons; invite skeptics to observe wins, not promises.

With a map, you move from improvisation to choreography. People who feel seen show up differently. They bring solutions, not obstacles. They lend their reputations to your effort because you respected theirs. The agent reaches production not only intact but welcomed. That welcome is the difference between a tool that works and a tool that wins. "When they showed up with my concerns already addressed, and my language in the controls, the answer was easy." – Chief Risk Officer, FTSE-50 insurer.

Principle 26: Stage the Win

Definition: Use agent wins to create executive theater.

In corporate environments, victories are not self-evident. Victories are carefully staged, framed, and communicated in ways that amplify their perceived value. "Staging the win" for AI agents means deliberately curating the moment of success so that it resonates at the right altitude in the organization. This is not about manipulation; it is about ensuring that achievement translates into influence. The staging process starts long before the win itself. It involves setting expectations, identifying the right audience, and preparing the narrative so that when the moment arrives, stakeholders not only see the success, but they also feel ownership of it. Without staging, even a transformative outcome risks fading into the noise of quarterly operations. With it, a single milestone can become a catalyst for executive sponsorship, budget expansion, and cultural momentum.

Why It Matters to Corporations: Small victories must be showcased. Behavioral science proves visible wins build momentum, and executives support proven results. Carefully orchestrating early successes creates psychological buy-in, excitement, and investment. Agent performance unseen is agent power unrealized. Stage early wins theatrically. In politics, policy wins are staged to capture public imagination; in business, transformation wins must be staged to secure political capital. AI agents, no matter how effective, struggle to gain attention amid competing priorities, fluctuating market conditions, and limited leadership bandwidth. An unplanned win risks going unnoticed. From a behavioral science perspective, staging a win leverages the "peak-end rule," a psychological effect in which people remember peak moments and endings more vividly. Suppose the first visible result of the adoption process is presented as a peak moment. In that case, it shapes how they remember the initiative as a whole because they've seen it succeed publicly.

Real-World Example: At a Fortune 200 industrials company, a route optimization agent reduced delivery times by 14% in a key metro area. The operational improvement was notable, but the crucial moment occurred when the COO conducted a live comparison during the quarterly strategy meeting. Two identical shipments, one planned by the agent and the other by a traditional method, were tracked in real time. The agent's shipment arrived two hours earlier. The room erupted in celebration. The win was now a shared experience, witnessed by the company's top 30 leaders. Within three months, the agent was rolled out nationally, not because the ROI spreadsheet was compelling (though it was), but because the staged win had become an internal legend. In the life of an AI agent, uncelebrated victories are squandered opportunities. A staged win converts operational success into political momentum, the fuel required for scaling. Leaders must treat staging as a deliberate act, not an afterthought.

Principle 27: Win the Gatekeeper

Definition: Win over the functional leader, adoption will follow.

Every company has *gatekeepers*, key leaders who control access to resources, influence adoption decisions, and shape organizational culture. In the context of AI agents, "winning the gatekeeper" means gaining the support of these influential figures before trying widespread deployment. Gatekeepers are not always the highest-ranking executives; they are often department heads, compliance leads, or operational directors whose approval can accelerate adoption or whose resistance can quietly kill momentum. Winning them requires demonstrating direct value to their function, aligning with their KPIs, and respecting their authority over domain expertise. Resistance from influential leaders halts deployments instantly. Identifying gatekeepers and winning their support through personalized incentives ensures smooth adoption and removes friction before it occurs. Gatekeepers can either shut down or accelerate agents. Win them, and the rest follow by default.

Why It Matters to Corporations: In large corporations, bypassing a gatekeeper to push technology adoption is a political misstep. Even with top-level sponsorship, an uncooperative gatekeeper can delay rollouts, slow budget approvals, or seed skepticism among their teams. Behavioral science calls this the "ego-affirmation effect." People are more receptive to change when their expertise and status are acknowledged. AI agents should be seen not as replacements for the gatekeeper's oversight, but as tools that enhance their effectiveness and influence in their role.

Real-World Example: A European retail bank attempted to roll out an AI-driven compliance monitoring agent without first securing the head of compliance's full support. While the agent's technology was sound, the compliance chief felt bypassed and subtly discouraged adoption across her teams. After six months of stalled progress, the project team reset the approach. They invited the compliance head into the design phase, allowed her to shape the alert thresholds, and positioned the agent as a direct enabler of her quarterly regulatory reports. Within eight weeks, she became the most vocal advocate for adoption, personally presenting the agent's impact to the executive committee. Gatekeepers are accelerators or bottlenecks; there is no middle ground. Winning them is not a courtesy; it is a prerequisite for sustained adoption.

Principle 28: Win the Frontline

Definition: Build emotional buy-in with frontline teams.

Frontline employees who will interact with the AI agent daily are the most critical group for adoption. Earning their trust and emotional commitment ensures engagement. Conversely, resistance from these employees can undermine even the most well-funded initiatives. Winning the frontline first means involving these teams early, listening to their concerns, and visibly incorporating their feedback. It's about demonstrating, through the agent's design and performance, that the agent matters to them by simplifying their work rather than complicating it.

Why It Matters to Corporations: Cultural adoption cascades upward from the frontline. When employees who directly operate the system endorse it, they generate grassroots credibility that no executive memo can replicate. Behavioral science underscores the importance of "self-determination theory," which suggests that people support tools that enhance their competence, autonomy, and relatedness. An agent who feels imposed upon and unhelpful will trigger resistance behaviors, such as workarounds, passive disengagement, or outright rejection. An agent that empowers will inspire champions at the grassroots level. Frontline endorsement also creates resilience. When leadership changes or budgets tighten, agents beloved by frontline teams often survive because removing them would create operational backlash.

Real-World Example: A global consumer goods company introduced a demand forecasting tool to its sales teams. Instead of a top-down rollout, the pilot started with a small group of high-performing sales reps who helped shape the interface and outputs. These reps became strong advocates, sharing their positive experiences informally with colleagues. When the company scaled the agent, adoption rates were 30% higher in regions where these early champions worked, and feedback cycles improved because the frontline felt ownership of the tool's success. Frontline teams are the ultimate litmus test for agent viability. Winning them early builds momentum that formal communication plans cannot match. Frontline teams are force multipliers, not just end users.

Chapter 4 Conclusion

Deploying AI agents is not just an engineering challenge; it's about wielding influence. By following these principles, you gain narrative control, strategically frame status, and effectively persuade stakeholders, guiding projects from mere proposals to implemented policies. Without alignment and advocacy, deployments can stall, but with them, agents become truly transformative.

Key Takeaways

- AI agents thrive when they serve as force multipliers for human leadership, doing the heavy lifting while allowing executives to own the strategic narrative.
- Mission-critical positioning is non-negotiable. Agents framed as optional inevitably lose funding and influence.
- Political intelligence drives adoption mapping, stakeholder engagement, winning over gatekeepers, and securing frontline buy-in to create a stable base of support.
- Narrative framing is just as vital as technical ability; leaders must understand the "why" and "how" of agent deployment to ensure alignment with the larger agenda.
- Orchestrated wins amplify influence. And visible, staged victories turn technical success into organizational momentum.

AI adoption begins with leadership endorsement, is reinforced by stakeholder trust, and gains permanence through visible, undeniable results.

Adopting AI agents in business is as much about politics as it is about technology. Success depends on matching agent capabilities with leadership goals and shaping organizational perception. AI agents become indispensable when they relieve operational burdens, accelerate decision-making, and deliver results that leadership can claim as their own. The guiding principle here is that agents survive by securing political sponsorship. Every adoption, from the executive offices to the factory floor, tests influence. AI adoption begins with leadership endorsement, is reinforced by stakeholder trust, and gains permanence through visible, undeniable results. The most sustainable adoptions aren't always the most technically advanced, but rather those that frame agents as part of leadership's achievements. Staged rollouts build momentum that raw technical merit alone cannot create. In corporate life, optics, political capital, and the ability to translate technical wins into strategic advantages matter. Leaders must ask: *Does our AI agenda reinforce our influence, or simply chase innovation?* Every decision about presenting and scaling agents impacts your political standing. For AI champions, remember: adoption succeeds through persuasion, not force. Agents must win support before they win funding. Understand the power networks, celebrate early victories, and ensure agents extend leadership rather than compete with it. Success is less about technical prowess and more about building alliances, earning influence, and orchestrating visible wins. Treat each deployment as an exercise in coalition-building, and your agents will help shape your business's future.

Persona Highlights

Jordan, Chief Strategy & Transformation Officer

- Anchors on "Map the Power" and "Stage the Win."
- *Key takeaway:* Must choreograph adoption as a political campaign, spotlighting wins as proof points for the board.

Claire, Chief Financial Officer

- Resonates with "Essential, Not Extra."
- *Key takeaway:* Agents must be positioned as indispensable for delivering financial strategy, not discretionary spend.

Rafael, Chief Technology Officer

- Aligns with "Make It Serve, Not Steer."
- *Key takeaway:* Agents must reinforce the enterprise strategy to avoid appearing as autonomous systems.

Simone, Chief Human Resources Officer

- Sees "Agents Lift Leaders" and "Win the Frontline" as cultural imperatives.
- *Key takeaway:* Adoption depends on leaders feeling amplified and employees feeling empowered.

Mo, Chief Marketing Officer

- Energized by "Stage the Win."
- *Key takeaway:* Leverage marketing to amplify agent victories that accelerate both internal momentum and external brand leadership.

Chapter 5

Innovation, Ecosystem, and Adaptability

AI agents do not operate in static environments; they exist within volatile ecosystems where expectations change, technology advances, and politics intervene. This chapter addresses the agent's adaptability, modularity, and strategic embeddedness, three factors that determine long-term survival and impact. Using behavioral science triggers like reciprocity, curiosity gaps, and identity reinforcement, the principles in this chapter help you re-architect not just the tools, but also the operating model around them. When agents adapt faster than the organization, they signal power. When the organization adapts to the agents, they become a permanent structure. Innovation that survives scale is rarely a single breakthrough; it is a system that learns, responds, and reconfigures itself as the business moves. Chapter 5 is about building that system. In fast markets, scripts age overnight, hero processes become liabilities, and yesterday's best practice can be tomorrow's bottleneck. The agents that matter are those who learn while they work, react in real time, and reshape the operating model based on what they prove. They start where the pain is sharpest, they scale the cure with discipline, and they refuse to idolize yesterday's roles when new capabilities can carry the load. Above all, they are designed to drift with the shifts we know are coming in customers, regulations, economics, and strategies.

What follows is a disciplined approach to adaptive advantage: small loops, short lags, clear ownership, and a bias to measurable outcomes. As one COO put it after the first quarter of agent-led operations, "We stopped managing by stories and started managing by signals." That is the center of gravity for this chapter: fewer declarations, more signals; fewer scripts, more decisions at the edge; fewer static roles, more accountability tied to outcomes. Use these principles to build an ecosystem that keeps getting better as your agents, processes, and people learn together.

DOI: 10.4324/9781003749899-9

Principle 29: Recode the Org DNA

Definition: Reinvent the operating model around agents.

In any enterprise, the "organizational DNA" is the invisible code dictating how decisions are made, how work is valued, how accountability is assigned, and how success is measured. It is embedded in reporting lines, approval chains, incentive systems, and even cultural norms. When this DNA is designed for an era of manual execution, retrofitting AI agents into it is akin to splicing advanced genetic material into a body that rejects the transplant, and it may even trigger bigger rejection. Rewriting the DNA is a fundamental act of renewal. It does not mean discarding everything that works; it means altering the blueprint so that the business treats AI agents not as visiting contractors, but as native contributors to the enterprise's functioning. This involves rethinking decision rights (what agents can decide autonomously vs. where human oversight is required), altering workflows to exploit 24/7 digital execution, aligning KPIs to measure agent impact, and redesigning incentives. Hence, human teams see agents as force multipliers, not threats. In this recoded model, agents and humans share the enterprise metabolism. Agents become embedded in the chain of value creation, and every process is re-architected to play to their strengths: consistency, scalability, speed, and integration across silos. Humans, freed from repetitive execution, can focus on interpretation, creativity, and relationship-building. Without recoding the DNA, AI agents are condemned to remain surface-level tools that produce local efficiencies but never trigger enterprise-scale transformation. "Recode the Org DNA" is the move from bolt-on to built-in. Instead of fitting agents into legacy swim lanes, you redefine roles, rhythms, and controls so the default way of working assumes agents exist. It touches structure (who owns what), processes (who starts, who decides, who reviews), and measures (what we count, who gets credit). The goal is to remove the friction that comes from treating agents as foreign bodies and replace it with an operating model where human judgment and machine leverage are interlocked.

Why It Matters to Corporations: Bolt-on solutions can stall progress. People revert to old paths. Costs creep. By recoding, you capture the full value: fewer handoffs, clearer decision rights, faster cycles, and budgets that move from "innovation" to operations. A corporation that fails to recode its DNA risks three strategic failures:

1. **Trapped Value:** Agents assigned to legacy processes often inherit inefficiencies rather than eliminate them.
2. **Cultural Resistance:** Humans cling to old operating patterns, creating friction that limits adoption.
3. **Strategic Stagnation:** Leadership underestimates what agents can deliver, budgeting them as marginal tools rather than transformational assets.

Recoding solves this by:

- Embedding agents in governance so their outputs are trusted and acted upon without excessive human gatekeeping.
- Integrating agents into cross-functional workflows, enabling faster execution and decision-making across silos.
- Redefining performance metrics to reward teams for leveraging agents effectively, rather than hoarding manual tasks for control.
- Structuring career paths where working with agents is a leadership competency, not a peripheral skill.

Behavioral science reinforces this need: people adopt change when it is embedded into default choices, reinforced socially, and rewarded tangibly. When the DNA changes, agent usage becomes the norm, not the exception.

Real-World Example: A North American health system recoded its prior-authorization process around an agent. Old: five handoffs, variable criteria, clinician interruption. New: single intake, agent triage with clear rules, nurse practitioner final say on exceptions, clinician time protected. They created new roles (authorization coach, agent owner), new rhythms (twice-weekly rule tuning), and new measures (clinician-interruption minutes avoided). Results: 41% faster turnaround, 18% fewer clinician pings, and the budget moved from pilot to operating line. Recode or regress. Make the new way unavoidable and rewarding:

- Write the new playbook, org chart, RACI, cadence, and metrics.
- Decommission legacy steps. Don't let shadow processes persist.
- Pay for outcomes. Shift incentives to results achieved in the new model.
- Institutionalize ownership. A named leader runs the agent as a product.

Do this, and "how we work" changes not just "what tool we use." Recoding organizational DNA is an executive act of redefinition. It signals to every stakeholder that agents are not experiments, but contributors to the enterprise's future. Without this step, AI transformation is cosmetic. With it, transformation becomes compounding. Executives must be explicit: agent integration is not optional, and the operating model will evolve to maximize their value. This creates an environment where agents and humans can elevate one another, mutually enhancing the enterprise's performance and resilience.

Principle 30: Reinvent, It's a New Day

Definition: Agents assume new roles and don't perpetuate the past.

When organizations initially implement AI agents, the tendency is to replicate familiar workflows and replace them 1:1 with traditional job roles. Where this approach is straightforward and secure, it is strategically flawed. Your current job roles were designed for the constraints of their era: limited data, slower decision cycles, and human cognitive bandwidth. Retrofitting agents into these molds forces them to inherit outdated assumptions. You get incremental improvement, not transformation. Instead, net-new roles must be designed from first principles:

- What can agents do that was previously impossible?
- How should decision rights change when speed, scale, and accuracy are no longer limiting factors?
- How can human effort be redeployed to areas that most benefit from empathy, judgment, and creativity?

This is the time for reimagination. There's no need to limit an agent's potential to old business models. Not only should you avoid designing an agent against broken processes, but there's also no need to create agents based on legacy job roles just because "this is how we've always done it."

Why It Matters to Corporations: Retrofitting agents into outdated roles introduces three silent killers of transformation:

1. Agents become mere task-automators, instead of opportunity creators.
2. Legacy workflows remain dominant, delaying the shift to an AI-optimized model.
3. Employees view agents as marginal upgrades rather than revolutionary tools, fostering cultural complacency.

Designing entirely new roles unlocks hidden enterprise potential. Think of the leap from paper ledgers to ERP systems: the real value emerged when companies redesigned processes to leverage real-time data, not merely digitized old forms.

Real-World Example: A major U.S. telecom giant began its AI transformation by replicating existing call-center workflows. Early conversational agents handled billing and troubleshooting but mainly mimicked legacy functions, resulting in some efficiency gains without true innovation. The breakthrough came when leadership shifted their perspective from, "How can AI handle more calls?" to "What can an AI agent do that no human ever could?" This prompted a comprehensive overhaul, including the creation of the customer signal agent, an AI-first layer integrating analytics, behavioral science, and intelligent orchestration. Instead of merely responding to inquiries, agents anticipated intent across 170 million customer interactions, resolving issues like outages or payment friction before customers reached out. Traditional roles were reimagined: supervisors became AI behavior trainers, auditors became experience stewards, and human agents took on complex, empathy-driven "escalations." In 18 months, 80% of inquiries were resolved autonomously, customer churn decreased by 100,000, and Net Promoter Scores rose significantly. Success was now measured by trust and prevention, rather than handle time. A new role, the customer intelligence designer, bridged data science with empathy to ensure the AI enhanced human abilities. By avoiding the trap of retrofitting old roles, the company transformed its contact center into a predictive loyalty engine, exemplifying Principle 30: "Reinvent, It's a New Day."

Leaders need the courage to redesign, not just retrofit. The payoff is twofold: agents achieve their full potential, and humans are elevated to more meaningful work.

Principle 31: Spot the Sore, Scale the Cure

Definition: Find the pain point the agent will solve, then amplify it.

"Spot the sore" is the disciplined act of identifying a business pain point so acute that solving it will deliver undeniable value. "Scale the cure" is the strategy of expanding that solution across the enterprise until the gains multiply. AI agents fail most often when they are deployed to low-impact or politically insignificant problems. The stakes are too low for leadership attention, and the results, however positive, go unnoticed. By contrast, when you target a sore point felt across the organization, such as a chronic bottleneck, a compliance risk, or a profit leak, the cure becomes headline-worthy. Scaling the cure involves designing the agent's capabilities to be generalized, followed by methodically integrating them into adjacent processes, business units, or geographies. This creates a flywheel effect: the more the cure is applied, the more the organization trusts, funds, and champions agents.

Why It Matters to Corporations: Corporations face dozens of pain points at any given time, but only a handful are "value-dense" where fixing them changes the economics of the business. Targeting these first has several strategic advantages:

- **Instant Credibility:** Solving a high-profile problem earns agents legitimacy in the eyes of leadership and the front line.
- **Momentum for Adoption:** Early, visible wins create social proof and reduce skepticism.
- **Funding Acceleration:** Finance leaders are far more willing to scale a proven cure than to continue funding pilots.
- **Change Management Leverage:** A well-chosen sore point rallies multiple functions behind the solution, creating cross-silo alignment.

From a behavioral science perspective, the human brain is wired to remember extremes, such as big wins or significant failures. If your first cure is a high-impact win, you lock in a narrative of competence and inevitability.

Real-World Example: A global logistics firm was facing mounting penalties for delayed customs documentation. This was costing $42 million annually in fees and lost contracts. The AI team identified this as the sore point. An agent was deployed to extract shipping data, auto-populate customs forms, and flag anomalies in real time. Within six months, penalties dropped by 85%. The CFO championed scaling the cure: the same agent architecture was adapted for invoicing, regulatory reporting, and insurance claims. Within 18 months, the company saved $120 million, and agents were viewed as a competitive differentiator. Spotting the sore and scaling the cure are political and economic accelerants for AI adoption. Leaders who take this route make agents unavoidable in strategic conversations because the results are too significant to ignore. The discipline lies in resisting the temptation to scatter agent deployments too thinly. Focus on one sore, cure it, and then turn that cure into a platform. In doing so, you turn every success into a lever for greater transformation.

Principle 32: Live Learning Loops

Definition: Deploy agents that learn while they work.

"Live Learning Loops" means your agents improve in production, not just in the lab. It is the practice of embedding structured feedback, evaluation, and controlled updates into an agent's daily operations so that each interaction informs the next. The live loop is concrete: observe → evaluate → adjust → verify → release.

Observe means instrumenting the agent to capture inputs, decisions, outcomes, and user corrections. Evaluate means scoring those decisions against business-grounded criteria, such as accuracy, cost, compliance, and customer impact. Adjust means applying small, controlled changes, such as prompt edits, rule tweaks, retrieval updates, or model fine-tuning, to improve the score. Verify

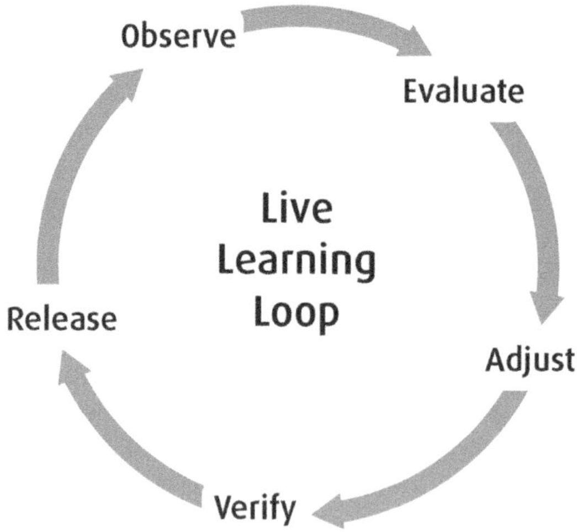

Figure 5.1 Live learning loop. Diagram by BMO Financial Group.

means checking the change against holdouts and guardrails. Release means promoting the improvement with rollback ready. A live loop is not "learn everything from everyone." It is specific and safe. You define which signals matter (e.g., "was the claim routed correctly?"), who can label or correct (frontline users with lightweight controls; experts for thorny cases), and how often can changes be shipped (daily prompt rotations, weekly retrieval refreshes, monthly model updates). You also define no-go zones: data that must not be used, decisions that must remain human, and threshold events that trigger pause and review. Technically, live loops rely on telemetry (decision logs, feedback APIs), evaluation suites (golden sets, scenario tests), and a small "release train" that moves improvements through development, staging, and production with versioning. Organizationally, they rely on clear ownership: a product owner who decides what "better" means; a risk partner who validates guardrails; and a design partner who keeps feedback effortless. Politically, they rely on transparency: publish what changed and why, so trust grows with improvement.

Why It Matters to Corporations: Corporations win by compounding advantages. Static systems are effective once, but learning systems improve every week. Live learning loops compound three kinds of advantage:

1. **Performance Advantage:** Markets shift quickly, with prices, fraud patterns, demand curves, and regulations changing rapidly. Agents that learn in production re-fit to reality before quarterly reviews catch up. Minor prompt adjustments informed by frontline corrections can lift accuracy without the cost or risk of full retraining. Retrieval updates can reflect new policy language within hours, not weeks. Over a year, these small, safe moves produce step changes: fewer escalations, shorter cycle times, and higher first-pass yields.
2. **Political Advantage:** When users see their corrections change the system, they feel a sense of ownership. That shifts posture from compliance to contribution. Executives gain confidence because improvement is visible, recorded, and tied to outcomes. Risk leaders gain leverage because updates run through a predictable cadence with pre-defined tests. The narrative flips from "AI is brittle" to "AI is responsive." That narrative is capital used to secure the budget and weather mistakes.
3. **Economic Advantage:** Every avoidable rework costs margin. Learning loops target specific error patterns that create rework and remove them first. Over time, your cost to serve drops while your service quality rises. The economics become predictable because you are not betting on rare "big bang" upgrades; you are banking steady, explainable gains. CFOs prefer this: improvements they can plan, not miracles they must hope for.

Behavioral science strengthens the case. Commitment and consistency: when you ask for small, easy feedback and show it matters, people keep engaging. Variable reward: seeing some changes land quickly makes the loop feel alive, increasing participation. Cognitive fluency: when the agent's responses increasingly match how users think and speak, trust rises. Your loop not only changes the model but also alters the relationship between people and the system. Governance is where learning loops are won or lost. Without guardrails, loops can drift into bias, data leakage, or unintended behavior. With guardrails, loops become audit-friendly. Define (a) what can change automatically (e.g., prompt phrasing), (b) what requires review (e.g., retrieval corpus updates), and (c) what requires formal approval (e.g., model fine-tunes in regulated flows). Publish your "change log" tightly: date, change, reason, test results, and owner. Compliance likes clarity. So do executives. Finally, learning loops create organizational memory. The "lessons" are encoded in prompts, rules, retrieval, and test suites, outliving staff changes and preserving gains through leadership transitions. You are no longer reliant on who remembers what; the system remembers. "The moment my team saw their corrections change next week's behavior, adoption took off. It felt like coaching a colleague, not fighting a tool." – VP Claims Operations, Fortune 200 insurer.

Real-World Example: A multinational online grocer deployed a fulfillment-prioritization agent to cut late deliveries. In the first month, the agent misprioritized specific bulk orders on rainy days, leading to van capacity being clogged. Rather than freeze rollouts, the team activated the live learning loop.

1. **Observe:** Drivers flagged "late risk" stops with a two-tap mobile control; the system logged weather, load mix, route geometry, and driver notes.
2. **Evaluate:** A weekly suite measured "promised vs. delivered window," "van utilization," and "customer complaint rate," segmenting by weather and order mix.
3. **Adjust:** The team added a weather-sensitive constraint to the route scorer and updated the retrieval corpus to reflect the latest dispatch.
4. **Verify:** A/B ran across three depots; guardrails checked that small-item orders were not starved.
5. **Release:** Changes shipped to all depots with a one-page document titled "What Changed and Why."

Within six weeks, late deliveries fell 23%, van utilization rose 8%, and driver satisfaction ticked up ("fewer impossible routes"). The CFO noticed the predictable weekly improvements: "This is an improvement we can budget on." The learning loop, not a model swap, delivered the win. Learning loops are not a feature; they are your operating model. They make improvement habitual and safe. To institutionalize:

- Define "better": Choose 3–5 outcome metrics your sponsor already reports (e.g., first-pass yield, time to resolution).
- Make feedback effortless: Two taps, one short field, or a "thumbs with reason" that takes seconds.

- Ship in small units: Weekly prompt/retrieval updates; monthly larger changes. Publish the change log.
- Guard the gate: Classify changes by risk; automate the low, review the medium, approve the high.
- Close the loop visibly: Inform users about the changes they've made. It is how you earn the subsequent correction.

When you work this way, agents gain a reputation for responsiveness; leaders gain confidence that the system won't stagnate; and risk becomes traceable. You stop waiting for a perfect model and start sustaining a better system. That posture, steady and governed, turns AI from a project into a practice the enterprise knows how to run.

Principle 33: React in Real-Time

Definition: Let agents respond in real-time, not scripts.

"React in Real-Time" means your agents respond to events as they happen, not after reports are pulled or scripts are executed on a schedule. It is the difference between closing the barn door and holding the door while the horse stays inside. Real-time is not heart-stopping speed for its own sake; it is decision latency that aligns with business reality. Fraud interdiction can take seconds, inventory reallocation may take minutes, and credit repricing could take hours. The principle aims to eliminate stale lag that destroys value. Technically, this requires event-driven architecture: streaming inputs (transactions, sensor data, user actions), stateless or lightly stateful processing, and policies that trigger actions (block, route, alert, price). It demands SLOs (service-level objectives) for detection and action, and graceful degradation when upstream systems slow down. It requires explainability under time pressure; you must quickly explain why the decision was made to maintain trust and meet audit requirements. Organizationally, real-time requires clear decision rights at the edge: what the agent can do immediately, what it can propose, and what it must escalate. It needs runbooks for incident conditions and throttles to avoid runaway behavior. Politically, it needs sponsors who value prevention as much as postmortem leaders willing to shift the meeting from "what happened?" to "what just happened and what did we do?"

Why It Matters to Corporations: Much of an enterprise's value evaporates in the gap between detection and action. Fraud, outage cascades, stockouts, and social blowups are most likely to worsen by the minute. Real-time agents shrink that gap.

- **Revenue and Loss:** In payments, blocking a suspicious transaction before authorization is categorically different from chasing a chargeback. In e-commerce, nudging a save-offer during checkout beats sending an apology email tomorrow. When your agent reacts in the moment, your P&L feels it directly.

- **Customer Trust:** Customers remember interventions that saved them by stopping a fraudulent charge, helped them rebook during an airline irregular ops event, or notified them of a service degradation before they noticed. These are loyalty-defining moments. Agents that act in real time create disproportionately positive memories.
- **Operational Stability:** Many failures propagate. A late upstream step triggers overtime, misses windows, and causes rework. Real-time routing, queuing, and throttling minimize cascades. Less firefighting means less burnout, fewer tickets, and lower performance variance.
- **Political Capital:** Executives earn reputations for command of the moment. Dashboards with yesterday's truths are too late. When an agent quietly averts a visible incident, the sponsor's credibility rises. That credibility is convertible to budget and runway for the next deployment.
- **Regulatory Posture:** In regulated contexts, early detection and containment can be the difference between a reportable event and a near miss. Real-time controls, along with logged decisions and overrides, show regulators that you are in control.

Behavioral science helps explain the impact: peak-end rule (people remember intense moments), availability bias (leaders overweight recent, vivid events), and loss aversion (preventing loss feels powerful). Real-time wins punch above their statistical weight in shaping narratives. That is useful and ethical if tied to real outcomes. The trade-offs are real. Real-time systems cost more to operate, false positives can annoy customers, and over-automation can surprise teams. The answer is tiered real-time: act immediately when the cost of delay exceeds the cost of error; propose immediately when human confirmation adds value; log only when visibility is enough. Establish SLOs for detection and action; measure false positive/negative rates; create escape hatches (one-tap overrides, hold-queues). Publish a latency policy: where seconds matter, where minutes suffice, where hours are fine. "We shifted from weekly alert reviews to live interdiction with human confirmation on high-value cases. Losses dropped; morale improved. People prefer solving problems now." – Head of Fraud, Global payments company.

Real-World Example: A global payments network faced rising card-not-present fraud. Historically, analysts reviewed batches of alerts daily. By then, the funds were gone, and the damage to the reputation was set in. The firm implemented a real-time agent for authorization. The system streamed transaction features (merchant, amount, velocity, device, history) into an event-driven scorer. Policy tiers were defined as follows:

- **Tier 1 (instant block):** extreme risk patterns (impossible travel + device clone + velocity spike).
- **Tier 2 (challenge):** step-up authentication or soft decline with a retry path.
- **Tier 3 (notify human):** high-value, borderline cases queued with explanation.

All decisions have logged reasons. SLO: <150ms additional latency. Human analysts monitored drift and tuned rules weekly. Outcomes in three months: fraud loss rate down 37%; false positive declines stable within tolerance; customer satisfaction improved ("I was asked to confirm; it felt protective"). The CRO's update to the board shifted from historical charts to a one-pager: "What changed, what we stopped, and where we're tuning next." Real-time reaction did not eliminate fraud; it changed the slope. Real-time isn't a trophy; it is targeted speed where speed pays. To embed:

- **Map latency to value.** Decide where seconds, minutes, and hours matter. Align SLOs.
- **Tier actions.** Block, challenge, propose, or log by risk and value.
- **Instrument explanations.** Capture "why" with each decision to protect trust and audit.
- **Run books and throttles.** When inputs spike or models drift, know how to slow, pause, or escalate.
- **Review rhythms.** Weekly tuning with risk and ops; monthly architecture health checks.

Do this and "real-time" becomes a business capability, not a buzzword. You earn stories of prevention that bolster sponsorship and calm regulators. You spend fewer cycles apologizing and more cycles improving. The organization has learned that it can now manage, not just survive.

Principle 34: Design for Drift

Definition: Build agents that adapt as the business evolves.

Business is not static. Markets shift, regulations tighten, competitors innovate, and customer expectations evolve. In this environment, static agents designed for a single, fixed use case lose relevance almost immediately after deployment. Drift refers to the divergence that occurs over time between an agent's original design parameters and the dynamic reality of the business it serves. Data patterns change, workflows are re-engineered, policies are updated, and integration points migrate. Left unmanaged, this drift erodes performance, misaligns outputs, and undermines trust. Designing for drift means acknowledging that change is a condition to be engineered for from the outset, rather than dealing with it months after deployment when it silently occurs. To achieve this, enterprises must build AI agents with adaptation as a capability, not an afterthought. This involves:

- Modular architectures so components can be swapped or upgraded without complete rebuilds.
- Continuous learning loops to refine performance based on evolving datasets, user feedback, and contextual shifts.

- Flexible integrations that allow agents to plug into new systems, applications, or data sources as the technology stack changes.
- Governance frameworks that institutionalize monitoring, drift detection, and model refresh cycles as part of normal operations, making updating agents routine.

Just as ships are designed to adjust to tides and currents, agents must adapt to shifting business conditions without capsizing the value they deliver. When designed for drift, agents remain aligned with the enterprise's strategic direction. They evolve as regulations, markets, and business priorities evolve, protecting the return on intelligence already achieved and extending the agent's relevance across cycles of transformation. Designing for drift is, ultimately, planning for longevity: ensuring that intelligence compounds rather than decays as the organization advances.

Why It Matters to Corporations: Static agents create a false sense of security. Leaders see initial ROI and assume the value will persist, but without adaptability, these agents become less relevant over time. This is especially dangerous in industries with volatile regulatory landscapes or rapid innovation cycles, such as finance, health care, and logistics. Designing for drift turns agents from tactical assets into strategic infrastructure. They become part of the enterprise's change muscle, able to flex with new priorities rather than break under them. Behavioral science underscores why this matters: organizations often suffer from planning fallacies, underestimating the pace and scope of change. By engineering adaptability from the outset, you sidestep this bias and keep agents relevant longer.

Real-World Example: A retail chain launched an AI pricing agent tied directly to seasonal demand models. It worked brilliantly until the supply chain crisis hit, and the model failed to account for sudden product shortages. The next iteration was built for drift, featuring modular pricing logic, integrated supplier data feeds, and a governance rule requiring any agent more than six months old to be reviewed against current market conditions. When inflationary shocks hit the following year, the agent adapted automatically, maintaining margins without manual intervention. Designing for drift is an act of humility. It acknowledges that no matter how well you understand the business today, tomorrow will be different. Leaders who embrace this truth build agents that outlive product cycles, leadership changes, and market disruptions, ensuring AI remains a strategic asset, not a disposable experiment.

Chapter 5 Conclusion – Innovation, Ecosystem, and Adaptability

Principle: Agents Are Not Projects; They Are Ecosystems – Design for Adaptability.

When organizations view AI agents as isolated projects, they miss the larger point and potential. A project has a start and an end. An ecosystem, however, lives, evolves, and scales. The difference is fundamental. Projects fade with budget cycles; ecosystems endure and grow, compounding value over time.

Chapter 5 makes a bold statement: the future of AI belongs not to those who launch projects, but to those who nurture ecosystems. More than anything, they remind leaders that innovation is an operating system, not a one-time event, the continuous condition through which an enterprise earns its return on intelligence. The six principles in this chapter serve as a blueprint for embedding adaptability into the organizational DNA. They address resistance, the allure of legacy systems, and the need for ongoing learning.

The Ecosystem Doctrine

Taken together, these six principles reshape innovation. They shift the emphasis from isolated deployment to adaptive ecosystems, from nostalgia for legacy systems to future-oriented design, and from rigidity to resilience. An ecosystem approach reframes the role of leadership. It requires executives to shift their focus from measuring success in pilots to measuring it in the context of systemic adoption. It requires investment not just in technology, but also in rewiring governance, incentives, and talent models. It demands humility, acknowledging that drift is inevitable, and courage, allowing agents to reshape the enterprise continuously. The message of Chapter 5 is clear: adaptability is power.

Enterprises that design agents as ecosystems will outlast, outlearn, and outpace their competitors. Those who idolize yesterday, bolt on agents as projects, or ignore drift will fall victim to irrelevance. Innovation, then, is not a project plan. It is a living ecosystem, a discipline of continual alignment between intelligence and impact. Leaders who design for adaptability will reap the harvest. Those who do not will watch their projects wither. In practical terms, this means bypassing abstract ROI models and delivering irrefutable proof that an agent removes a business pain faster, cheaper, and better than any alternative. The temptation to idolize yesterday is seductive because it feels safe. Yet history is filled with market leaders who fell because they optimized for familiarity over potential. No matter how visionary the deployment, the half-life of relevance is shrinking. Build agents for drift, ensuring they evolve alongside the enterprise rather than calcify into relics of their launch context. Taken together, these principles demand a mindset shift: AI transformation is not a destination but an adaptive operating state. When organizations commit to the innovation discipline embedded in these six principles, they stop *implementing AI projects* and begin operating as adaptive intelligence systems, systems capable of learning, compounding, and regenerating value, the essence of a return on intelligence.

Persona Highlights

Jordan, Chief Strategy & Transformation Officer

- Anchors on "Recode the Org DNA" and "Design for Drift."
- *Key takeaway:* Agents must be embedded into the operating model to create an adaptive transformation that the board sees as sustainable.

Claire, Chief Financial Officer

- Resonates with "Spot the Sore, Scale the Cure."
- *Key takeaway:* Agents should target pain points that deliver measurable ROI, not vanity innovation.

Rafael, Chief Technology Officer

- Values "Live Learning Loops" and "React in Real-Time."
- *Key takeaway:* Agents must be designed as adaptive, resilient systems that evolve with workflows and customer needs.

Simone, Chief Human Resources Officer

- Sees "Reinvent, It's a New Day" as a cultural imperative.
- *Key takeaway:* Workforce design must evolve new roles, new skills, and new incentives rather than forcing agents into outdated constructs.

Mo, Chief Marketing Officer

- Energized by "Spot the Sore, Scale the Cure" and "React in Real-Time."
- *Key takeaway:* Agents must visibly improve the customer experience by addressing pain points and responding quickly to foster brand loyalty.

Part II Conclusion

When leadership alignment turns into an operational habit, transformation becomes irreversible. Agents cease to be projects competing for attention; they become doctrine guiding enterprise behavior. Leaders measure success not by volume of pilots but by the rate of institutional learning. At that point, intelligence stops being a function and starts being a culture. Momentum is intoxicating, but unchecked speed burns trust. Every agent that scales without governance becomes a risk multiplier. Part III is where leadership matures into stewardship. The question shifts from "How fast can we deploy?" to "How responsibly can we sustain?" Here, trust becomes the currency of scale.

Governance, transparency, and selective visibility transform adoption into credibility. We move from excitement to endurance, from scaling ambition to institutional confidence.

DOI: 10.4324/9781003749899-10

Part III

Governance

Trust, Transparency, and Scalable Momentum

Scale is not just a technical challenge; it is a trust challenge. Enterprises must design governance systems that protect confidence without paralyzing progress. Part III lays out how to institutionalize AI with precision and transparency, where selective disclosure builds trust, measurement reinforces credibility, and governance mechanisms transform risk into resilience (Chapter 6). Trust is not built by overexposure; it is built by consistency. When stakeholders see reliable outcomes, aligned incentives, and visible accountability, confidence compounds and is where return on intelligence becomes measurable (Chapter 7). Governance is the architecture of endurance.

DOI: 10.4324/9781003749899-11

Chapter 6

Trust, Transparency, and Selectivity

Trust is the currency that decides whether AI agents are accepted or rejected. Unlike apps or dashboards, agents function at the edge of visibility, making decisions, revealing truths, and prompting actions. That power comes with scrutiny. This chapter codifies how to design for psychological trust, drawing on principles from behavioral science such as selective disclosure, cognitive dissonance reduction, truth priming, and earned transparency. These principles help executives ensure agents are trusted not just for what they do, but also for how they do it and what they choose to reveal. Trust is the operating system of scale. In large enterprises, agents do not earn trust by explaining themselves endlessly; they earn it by producing outcomes that withstand scrutiny, by revealing the minimum necessary truth to the right people at the right time, and by declaring their limits before those limits declare themselves. When the stakes are high – regulatory exposure, customer safety, and market disclosures – transparency must be purposeful, not performative. Too much openness invites confusion, weaponized politics, or security risk. Too little invites suspicion and slow-rolling. The principles in this chapter draw that line and then enforce it. The purpose is pragmatic: to build a durable alliance among leaders, risk, and the frontline, stating "This system tells the truth we need, at the fidelity we can use, with the governance we can defend." Get that partnership right, and your agents will weather outages, vendor shifts, tough quarters, and leadership turnover. Get it wrong and you will be explaining yourselves while budgets move elsewhere. "We stopped trying to make the agent explain its soul. We made it prove its value and user trust followed." – Chief Risk Officer, Global 300 bank.

Principle 35: Outcomes Over Output

Definition: Let agents speak through outcomes, not explanations.

"Outcomes Over Output" means the primary evidence of an agent's value is the business result it delivers, not the volume of its responses, the elegance of

DOI: 10.4324/9781003749899-12

its prompts, or the depth of its model cards. In practical terms, the agent should be judged and funded on movements in the metrics your board and regulators already care about: capital, cycle time, error rate, loss avoidance, margin, safety incidents, customer experience, and audit findings. Explanations matter, but they are supporting documentation, not the product. The product is the outcome. This principle rejects two standard failure modes: first, explainability theater, which involves lengthy narratives about model architecture and prompt strategies that do not change decisions. Second, activity worship focuses on celebrating response counts, tokens used, or "engagement," while KPIs remain flat. Instead, the principle insists on a simple chain: define the outcome that matters; instrument the workflow so attribution is credible; report results in the language of finance, risk, and operations; maintain enough technical traceability to answer "why" when it matters. Design implications: dashboards present results first (e.g., "First-pass yield up 9.7% QoQ"), then short "how" notes for auditability. Review rhythms start with deltas, not demos. Executive theater shows before/after on a live KPI, not screenshots of clever prompts. Governance artifacts are crisp: data lineage, guardrails, and change logs are available when needed but remain invisible otherwise.

Why It Matters to Corporations: Enterprises run on credibility and capital. Capital flows to initiatives that move the P&L, reduce risk, and improve regulator posture. Credibility flows to leaders who keep promises. "Outcomes Over Output" serves both and promotes:

- **Budget Durability:** When the CFO sees consistent, audited improvements in cost-to-serve, loss rates, or cash conversion, the agent becomes a line-of-business infrastructure rather than a discretionary pilot. In downturns, infrastructure survives; pilots don't.
- **Political Safety:** Sponsors live in rooms where brevity and certainty are scarce. A one-pager that opens with outcome deltas ("chargeback losses −18%, false positives flat") gives them control. They can defend and extend the program without reciting technical detail and without fear that a probing question will expose soft ground.
- **Regulator Confidence:** Supervisors don't need to understand every weight and prompt; they need to see evidence of adequate controls and predictable outcomes. When your primary narrative is "here is the harm we prevented and the standard we meet," scrutiny narrows to scope and safeguards rather than existential doubt.
- **Cultural Clarity:** Frontline teams engage with tools that drive their performance. If the agent cuts handling time and reduces rework, word spreads. If it produces verbose explanations while work remains hard, cynicism spreads faster.
- **Vendor Leverage:** When outcomes are the contract currency, procurement negotiations are cleaner. You can switch models, change retrieval sources,

or replatform without destabilizing sponsorship because the business case is pinned to KPI movement, not a specific provider's mystique.

Behavioral science reinforces this stance: goal-gradient effect (people run harder when the goal is visible), salience (evident, relevant results command attention), and loss aversion (showing avoided loss motivates action more than abstract potential). Outcomes create a shared reality, a point of convergence for finance, risk, tech, and operations.

Real-World Example: A global metals and mining company initially introduced the application of an AI optimization system by its research and technology team to enhance operational efficiencies. The project languished in pilot mode for nearly a year, viewed as another digital experiment detached from day-to-day operations. That changed when the narrative shifted: the same model was reframed as a "*metallurgical recovery optimization tool*" directly accountable for maximizing copper recovery. Suddenly, it moved from a low-probability-of-success technology initiative to a revenue-generating lever under the COO's purview, working in close coordination with each mine's general manager. The pivot was subtle but transformational. The AI model analyzed thousands of variables across ore composition, crush size, throughput, and reagent levels to recommend real-time adjustments. Once those learnings were embedded in day-to-day operations, they unlocked a measurable 2% uplift in recovery rates, translating into significant, immediate revenue gains with virtually no additional operating or capital expenditures required. The same codebase, same algorithm, but reframed as a *production performance driver* rather than a "digital twin experiment." Given how closely recovery rates and production are monitored, the program's success was immediately evident throughout the organization. The AI tool gained legitimacy because it sat within the operational heartbeat of the business. The executive lesson is unmistakable: AI becomes transformative only when it's tethered to the P&L, not the proof-of-concept. This company didn't change its technology; it changed its sponsorship model. In mining, as in every sector, framing dictates adoption. When AI tools are owned by the people who own the outcome, such as COOs, CFOs, or mine general managers, they stop being experiments and start becoming engines that can extract tangible value. Make it muscle memory:

- In every forum (steerco, ELT, board), lead with outcome deltas tied to enterprise KPIs.
- Maintain a living "controls packet" (data lineage, guardrails, change log, evaluation suite) ready for deeper review.
- Reward teams for business movement, not "AI usage."
- Publish a quarterly "outcomes digest" to create social proof.

Over time, this posture changes how the organization thinks. Leaders stop asking, "What's the model?" and start asking, "What did it do that mattered?" Engineers stop optimizing for cleverness and start optimizing for impact. Risk stops fearing the unknown and starts partnering to make the known repeatable. The workforce experiences a tool that makes work easier, rather than a system that demands attention. In the boardroom, arguments are costly, and time is scarce. "Outcomes Over Output" respects both. It is about consistently converting capability into capital.

Principle 36: Hide the How

Definition: Hide the agent, spotlight the outcome.

In the enterprise boardroom, too much transparency is rarely rewarded; too little is never forgiven. "Hide the How" is the discipline of keeping the machinery out of the spotlight and centering the conversation on results. The premise is simple: executives, customers, and regulators care most about what the agent delivers, not how every component operates. The "how" is preserved, documented for governance, auditability, and engineering, but it is neither broadcast nor romanticized. This principle is not an argument for secrecy; it is an argument for selective transparency. The mechanics are made accessible to those who need to validate, control, or troubleshoot them, including risk managers, compliance officers, auditors, and system engineers. Everyone else sees the impact: cycle time is reduced, decision accuracy is improved, and customer wait time is shortened. Overexposure to the "how" can dilute confidence. Technical complexity invites unnecessary debate, politicization, and the temptation to micromanage. Meanwhile, operational and financial sponsors need a clean story they can defend without having to memorize the architecture of embeddings, fine-tuning pipelines, or vector databases. By spotlighting the outcome and keeping the operational choreography in the wings, you protect intellectual property, reduce the attack surface for critics, and ensure that accountability remains with people, not with opaque machinery.

Why It Matters to Corporations: In global enterprises, three dynamics make "Hide the How" vital:

1. **Boardroom Decision Velocity:** Senior leaders operate on compressed timelines. Their mental bandwidth is consumed by capital allocation, risk appetite, and competitive positioning. By focusing on outcome metrics, you align with their decision-making cadence and remove cognitive clutter.
2. **Risk and Regulatory Positioning:** Regulators are increasingly comfortable with layered transparency. A top-level assurance on outcomes, paired with a readiness to disclose technical details in controlled settings, builds confidence without oversharing operational blueprints.
3. **IP Protection and Vendor Leverage:** In multi-vendor environments, revealing too much of your architecture can weaken negotiation leverage or invite replication by competitors.

Behavioral science offers strong support for this approach: the information overload effect warns that surplus detail erodes clarity and decision quality; the anchoring effect shows that initial frames (e.g., outcome improvements) disproportionately shape perceptions; and the authority principle suggests that when results are backed by accountable leadership, trust is strengthened without exhaustive technical evidence. In practice, "Hide the How" creates cleaner governance rhythms. Executive steering packs open with three to five high-impact outcome metrics. Audit committees receive these metrics alongside targeted control evidence. Technical forums receive deeper architecture documentation as needed. This tiered structure provides each audience with the level of transparency appropriate to their role and no more.

Real-World Example: A Fortune 200 retail bank was rolling out an AI-powered loan decisioning agent. In the early pilot, the program team presented a 30-slide deck to the executive committee covering model architectures, data sources, and prompt engineering strategies. Interest was polite, but the funding decision stalled. The COO pivoted to the "Hide the How" posture. The new steering pack's first page displayed three key results:

1. Loan decision cycle time reduced by 42%.
2. Approval accuracy variance reduced from 3.5% to 1.2%.
3. Customer satisfaction with the decision experience improved by 18 points.

The "how" was summarized in one paragraph, with a note that the full technical details were on file with the risk committee. Regulatory stakeholders received the control documentation separately, while engineering maintained exhaustive internal records. The result? Funding was approved in ten minutes. The COO later noted "We did not get a single question on how the embeddings work because we led with proof that the business outcomes were in line with our strategy and controls were already signed off." The way you present the "how" isn't about hiding the truth; it's about timing it right. Lead with what makes an impact, then add assurance, and only reveal the details when they matter to the audience. This approach protects intellectual property, keeps the conversation strategic, and makes sure the story focuses on the business value the agent provides, not the technical details of the process. Practical commitments include:

- Tiering transparency by audience role.
- Leading all executive updates with three to five outcome metrics.
- Keeping technical detail in controlled, on-demand repositories.
- Training sponsors to answer confidently without diving into architecture.

Done well, this principle elevates the conversation from technology fascination to business conviction, where enterprise adoption decisions are made.

Principle 37: Reveal With Restraint

Definition: Share agent insights selectively to build trust.

"Reveal With Restraint" is the art of deciding who sees what, when, and why. In the age of AI, agents can produce vast streams of insights, correlations, and anomalies. Many of these are accurate, some are probabilistic, and a few are sensitive, controversial, or easy to misinterpret. The temptation is to share everything in the name of transparency. However, discipline requires sharing only what is relevant, actionable, and appropriate for the context. Selective disclosure helps prevent data manipulation, ensuring insights are used to support enterprise goals rather than for internal politics. It also supports regulatory compliance by ensuring that personally identifiable information, competitive intelligence, or risk-sensitive indicators are shared only with those who have a legitimate business need. Restraint is governance, whereby applying role-based access controls, aggregating data to safe levels before distribution, and sequencing insight release so that sponsors and teams can act before the information becomes a distraction or a liability.

Why It Matters to Corporations: Unfiltered insight flows create three enterprise hazards:

1. **Cognitive Overload**: Too much information, especially when mixed in quality and relevance, degrades decision speed and increases analysis paralysis.
2. **Security and Privacy Breaches**: Over-sharing sensitive or unvetted insight can expose the company to fines, litigation, or reputational damage.
3. **Organizational Mistrust**: Teams that receive raw, unexplained, or partial insights can lose confidence in the agent's reliability or the leadership's decision-making.

Behavioral science emphasizes restraint. The scarcity principle holds that selectively revealing information can boost perceived value and credibility. The context effect shows that understanding varies based on framing and timing. The trust asymmetry principle warns that misusing insight can destroy months of trust building. Companies that "Reveal With Restraint" create a culture where data is both trusted and utilized. This is achieved by setting insight tiers, for example:

- **Tier 1:** Executive-ready outcomes and risks (aggregated).
- **Tier 2:** Operational insights for mid-level managers (filtered by relevance).
- **Tier 3:** Raw insight streams for analysts and engineers (restricted access).

By clearly defining who gets which level, and why, the organization avoids accidental leaks, political misuse, and decision bottlenecks.

Real-World Example: A global pharmaceutical company deployed an agent to analyze R&D productivity across sites. The initial release sent raw performance dashboards to all senior scientists. Within weeks, political tensions erupted, and some teams used the data to undermine rivals rather than to improve the process. The program lead adopted "Reveal With Restraint." They created three views:

1. Executives received high-level trends and variance alerts by region.
2. Site leaders received filtered views relevant only to their location.
3. Analysts received the full dataset in a secure research environment.

The tone shifted. Instead of defensive emails, site leaders concentrated on their actionable metrics. Analysts still conducted deep correlations, but without causing political tension. To build trust during the design phase, practical commitments include defining audience tiers and matching insight details accordingly, aggregating and anonymizing data when necessary, sequencing insight releases to give accountable owners a first-mover advantage, and educating recipients on how to interpret and use the insights. Enterprises that master this principle avoid the two extremes of information hoarding and information dumping, instead creating a deliberate, credible flow that strengthens both adoption and governance.

Principle 38: Expose the Edges

Definition: Show your agent's limits before they fail publicly.

"Expose the Edges" requires you to declare and demonstrate where your agent should not be trusted before those boundaries are discovered the hard way, by a regulator, a customer, or a headline. An "edge" is any combination of input, context, or condition that materially degrades performance or raises risk beyond acceptable thresholds: low-representation data segments, long-tail intents, out-of-policy requests, novel fraud patterns, adversarial prompts, or operational load spikes. This principle has two halves. First, discovery: proactively stress-test the agent against realistic extremes using golden sets, red-team scenarios, chaos drills, and retrospective incident replay. Second, disclosure: communicate the edges to the relevant audiences, frontline users (tooltips, warnings), sponsors (risk heatmaps), risk/compliance (limits register), and customers where appropriate (policy disclosures). It also means instrumenting edge-handling: graceful degradation (route to human, request clarification, reduce scope), event logging, and recovery runbooks. Exposing edges is not self-sabotage; it is preemptive governance. You own the narrative, you protect users from brittle failure, and you build credibility with risk functions whose job is to imagine what could go wrong.

Why It Matters to Corporations: Reputation is a compound asset. One public failure at the edge can erase a year of quiet wins. "The day we published our limits deck internally, adoption improved. People finally knew when to lean in and when to call a human." – SVP Customer Operations, Global telco. This principle protects three fronts:

1. **Regulatory Posture:** Supervisors increasingly expect firms to understand and demonstrate model limitations, test coverage, and fallback designs. A crisp limits register with evidence of control performance shifts conversations from existential "Is this safe?" to operational "Is this governed?"
2. **Sponsor Credibility:** Executives are comfortable defending systems that admit uncertainty and demonstrate control. Sponsors lose face when a tool asserts confidence and then fails visibly. Declaring limits arms them with honest talking points and escape lanes.
3. **User Trust:** Frontline users forgive an agent who says, "I'm uncertain; here are options," especially when the fallback is fast. They do not forgive confident wrongness that creates rework, compliance exposure, or customer harm.

Behavioral science explains the effect: the pratfall effect (admitting a controlled flaw can increase perceived competence), the ambiguity reduction effect (clear boundaries reduce anxiety), and the anticipatory guidance effect (people manage risk better when told what to expect and what to do). By exposing edges, you lower cognitive load, increase perceived integrity, and improve adherence to safe use. Operationalizing the principle includes:

- **Edge Discovery Program:** Quarterly red-team exercises; synthetic long-tail generation; drift monitors; chaos tests (spikes, outages).
- **Limits Register:** For each edge include description, severity, detection method, guardrail, fallback, owner, evidence.
- **UX Patterns:** Soft warnings ("low confidence"), hard stops ("requires human review"), and one-click escalation with context.
- **Story Discipline:** Sponsor one-pagers include "Known Edges & Controls" to normalize the practice.

Real-World Example: A global airline deployed an irregular operations (IROPs) agent to rebook passengers during weather events. Early pilots looked strong until a regional storm exposed an edge: complex, multiple passenger name records (PNR) for multi-family bookings with mixed loyalty statuses. The agent rebooked partially, splitting families. Social blowback was immediate. The program pivoted to Expose the Edges. Discovery: replayed past storm days, created synthetic edge cases, and red-teamed adversarial prompts ("separate parties"). Disclosure: built a limits register, trained frontline staff with a two-minute "family booking edge" clip, and added a UX hard stop: "Mixed-status, multi-PNR detected, route to dedicated desk." Edge-handling: preserved soft benefits (waived fees) automatically while queuing for human resolution with full context. The next storm, rebooking net promoter score (NPS) held steady; social complaints dropped. The COO briefed the board with a slide titled "What We Learned and How We Control It." Credibility was restored because the team owned the edge and managed it effectively. Edges are predestined, but surprises are optional. Expose them, and you convert risk into managed variance. Hide them, and you convert variance into reputational debt. To institutionalize:

- Make edges a first-class artifact. Every agent has a limits register, which the product lead and risk partner own.
- Practice failure with quarterly chaos and red-team drills, including written lessons and shipped fixes.
- Normalize boundary language. Teach phrases like "low confidence," "fallback engaged," and "human-in-the-loop required."
- Report edges like outcomes. In steerco packs, pair KPI deltas with "edges discovered, controls deployed."

When leaders hear a clean story, "Here is where we are strong; here is where we are careful; here is how we respond," they back you. When regulators see disciplined boundary management, oversight lightens. Truth and trust compound, and users grow when users trust that the system will warn rather than bluff.

Principle 39: Limitations Fuel Innovation

Definition: Let legacy constraints reveal innovation opportunities.

At the enterprise scale, constraints are the creative brief. Legacy systems, regulatory guardrails, and entrenched workflows are often framed as barriers to AI adoption. Yet in practice, these limitations can serve as the boundaries that force ingenuity, accelerate adoption, and drive trust. When an AI agent is designed within the contours of a constraint, whether it is a compliance requirement, a legacy system dependency, or a customer expectation, it emerges more fit-for-purpose and less likely to face resistance. Constraints force prioritization. They sharpen design focus. They remove the temptation to create a generic, overbuilt agent that serves no one particularly well. This principle reframes "limitations" from being risk factors to being design catalysts. The friction points of the existing environment reveal where the most significant pain, and therefore the most tremendous potential for measurable value, lies. Legacy platforms might specify specific integration paths, compliance rules could restrict what can be automated, and workforce agreements may determine the speed of adoption.

Why It Matters to Corporations: Enterprise transformation teams often see constraints as obstacles to be "worked around" or "eliminated." This mindset wastes political capital and delays progress. A more strategic approach is to view constraints as co-designers. There are three reasons this is essential:

1. **Political Acceptance:** Stakeholders are more likely to approve an initiative that respects existing rules and dependencies, especially in the early phases.
2. **Regulatory Alignment:** Building within constraints demonstrates maturity and risk-awareness, which can accelerate regulatory sign-offs.
3. **Focused Innovation:** Scarcity sharpens creativity. Without unlimited freedom, teams innovate and produce targeted solutions that deliver outsized impact.

Scarcity sharpens creativity.

Behavioral science supports this idea: the creativity under constraint principle shows that boundaries enhance ideation; the mere-exposure effect suggests that solutions respecting existing norms are adopted more quickly. Additionally, the implementation intention framework indicates that specifying conditions ("If X constraint, then Y approach") improves follow-through. By framing constraints as intentional design choices rather than faults, leaders can shift conversations from "Why we cannot" to "Here's how we can."

Real-World Example: A Tier 1 European insurer struggled with a legacy mainframe system that couldn't be entirely replaced for at least five years. The claims department wanted an AI agent to triage incoming cases in real time, but complete system integration was impossible under current constraints. Instead of waiting for a future-state platform, the design team built an AI "sidecar" application that ingested mainframe output files every 15 minutes, analyzed claim types, and prioritized them for human review in a modern UI. The agent worked within and did not seek to eliminate the mainframe. The result was a 35% improvement in triage efficiency within 90 days, with no disruption to the legacy platform. The CIO later credited the mainframe's limitations for the team's avoidance of "scope bloat" and for delivering value quickly. The irony is that the same limitations executives initially see as constraints often become the scaffolding for sustainable transformation. When companies view constraints as inputs, they create more flexible agents, which builds the credibility needed for bolder moves later. Practical commitments include:

- Listing constraints during discovery as design inputs, not obstacles.
- Finding "constraint-compliant" quick wins to generate momentum.

- Sharing early wins as evidence that AI can succeed without dismantling the entire system.
- Using early credibility to negotiate for future constraint removal.

Principle 40: Expose With Accountability

Definition: Surface the uncomfortable truths, but own the stewardship of what happens next.

The primary responsibility of an AI agent is to represent reality as it is, not as stakeholders might wish. This means presenting facts honestly and without bias, avoiding language that could trigger defensiveness, and refraining from proposing solutions too soon, which could alienate decision-makers before they are prepared to listen. All of this must be done while upholding the ethical and political duty to make the truth both meaningful and actionable. In the corporate world, truth is a fragile asset. When handled well, it strengthens strategy, concentrates resources, and motivates decisive action. When mishandled, it can damage trust, spark resistance, or be used against those delivering it. "Expose With Accountability" demands a dual discipline: the agent must be unwavering in revealing data-driven realities and equally intentional in framing those revelations. Hence, they advance, not derail, the organization's agenda. This principle rejects two extremes: AI as a silent observer that withholds critical insights to avoid conflict, and AI as a reckless whistleblower that triggers chaos without owning the downstream consequences. The goal is to expose in a way that informs, engages, and equips leaders to act, preserving both the integrity of the insight and the relationships required to act on it.

Why It Matters to Corporations: In an enterprise AI transformation, the ability to surface uncomfortable truths is a competitive necessity. Strategic misalignment, inefficiency hotspots, policy non-compliance, or customer attrition patterns are the realities that must be illuminated early, before they metastasize into crises. Yet timing, context, and delivery determine whether that illumination drives improvement or fuels political resistance. Corporations are complex political ecosystems. Data points do not exist in a vacuum; they intersect with careers, budgets, and power structures. When AI agents expose performance gaps or compliance risks, they must do so in a way that preserves the organization's capacity to absorb the truth and respond constructively. From a behavioral science standpoint, humans resist information that threatens their self-concept, professional competence, or status. If an AI system exposes a failure without considering these human dynamics, stakeholders may reject the insight, not because it is inaccurate, but because the delivery felt like an ambush. By contrast, if the agent surfaces the truth with context, options for action, and respect for the decision-maker's authority, resistance diminishes and the likelihood of adoption rises dramatically. In governance terms, this principle aligns with responsible AI principles: fairness (avoiding selective or politically motivated exposure), accountability (ensuring apparent human oversight for how insights are acted upon), and transparency (clarifying the provenance of the data while safeguarding anonymity where necessary). It also strengthens political capital: leaders who see AI agents as fair brokers of truth rather than political actors are more likely to rely on them in high-stakes decisions.

Real-World Example: A global pharmaceutical company deployed AI agents to monitor clinical trial compliance. Early in the deployment, the system identified a high-risk protocol deviation in a flagship trial, which could potentially delay regulatory approval. The raw data was precise, but the AI team understood that presenting it bluntly and without filters could cause panic, internal blame, and harm to the project lead's reputation. Instead, the AI agent presented the finding as part of a broader compliance trend report, covering multiple sites and variables, not just the high-profile trial. It offered anonymized benchmarks and proposed mitigation options without identifying individuals. The insight was shared with the corporate risk committee, along with a discreet briefing for the trial lead. This approach kept the sense of urgency without leading to public scapegoating. The trial lead responded quickly, correcting the deviation within 48 hours, while the organization strengthened process controls across all trials. The agent maintained credibility as an impartial auditor, and leadership supported its ongoing use for real-time oversight. In a hybrid intelligence era where corporations are both data-rich and politically charged, the way an AI agent delivers truth determines whether that truth shapes policy or dies in silence. Exposure without accountability is as harmful as silence. It promotes intentional pacing, contextual framing, and respectful delivery of brutal truths, ensuring they act as catalysts for change rather than causing organizational stagnation. For executives, adopting this approach includes establishing clear protocols for revealing truths through agents, outlining escalation procedures, setting policies for anonymization, and developing framing strategies that preserve trust. It also means training human leaders to receive AI-derived truths without defaulting to defensiveness, so that insights become the foundation of competitive advantage rather than the spark for political infighting. The payoff is profound: corporations that can routinely confront uncomfortable truths, without fracturing trust, become exponentially more adaptive, resilient, and capable of sustaining strategic momentum in volatile markets.

Chapter 6 Conclusion – Trust, Transparency, and Selectivity

Principle: Trust Is Earned Through Restraint, Not Disclosure. Agents Must Inspire Confidence.

Trust in enterprise AI does not arrive by proclamation; it is earned incrementally, tested under constraint, and reinforced through consistent outcomes. In a corporate environment where technology can be both a disruptor and a scapegoat, the discipline of how an AI agent reveals, conceals, and positions itself determines whether it will become indispensable or disposable. Leaders who insist on revealing every technical detail risk drowning stakeholders in complexity or triggering unnecessary fear. Instead, effective agent governance means managing the flow of information with the precision of a diplomat enough to inspire confidence, not so much as to create confusion or suspicion. This chapter presents six principles of trust-building. Each principle acknowledges the paradox of AI adoption: people demand visibility, but too much visibility undermines confidence. Agents must therefore be managed with nuance, balancing accountability with restraint, disclosure with design. Together, these six principles redefine how trust is earned in the AI age. They replace naive transparency with strategic selectivity, replacing explanation with proof, concealment with accountability. The message is clear: trust is not a feature of the technology; it is a feature of leadership. Agents will not succeed because they are sophisticated. They will succeed because leaders orchestrated the perception of their credibility. Trust is political capital. Boards allocate funding when they trust. Employees adopt willingly when they trust. Customers stay loyal when they trust. Regulators restrain scrutiny when they trust.

In each instance, the balance is fragile. Leaders must manage the narrative carefully: spotlight outcomes, acknowledge edges, reveal selectively, and own the truth. This chapter positions trust as the ultimate differentiator. Competitors can replicate technology and have similar talent strategies, but competitors cannot easily replicate trust. Trust compounds, becoming reputation. And reputation, in turn, becomes market power. In the end, the greatest challenge of AI adoption is not technical; it is psychological. It is about whether leaders can create the conditions under which people believe. Those who follow these principles will transform agents from curiosities into confidants. Those who ignore them will face skepticism, resistance, and failure.

Persona Highlights

Jordan, Chief Strategy & Transformation Officer

- Anchors on "Outcomes Over Output" and "Expose With Accountability."
- *Key takeaway:* Trust builds transformation momentum when agents demonstrate measurable business outcomes and leaders own the narrative around failure.

Claire, Chief Financial Officer

- Resonates with "Reveal With Restraint" and "Expose the Edges."
- *Key takeaway:* Financial stewardship requires acknowledging agent limits upfront while providing the proper disclosures to maintain credibility with boards and regulators.

Rafael, Chief Technology Officer

- Values "Hide the How" and "Limitations Fuel Innovation."
- *Key takeaway:* Technology leaders should emphasize resilience and innovation born of constraints rather than overexplaining complexity.

Simone, Chief Human Resources Officer

- Sees "Outcomes Over Output" and "Reveal with Restraint" as cultural imperatives.
- *Key takeaway:* Employees will adopt agents more quickly if they trust the outcomes, understand guardrails, and feel psychological safety around limitations.

Mo, Chief Marketing Officer

- Energized by "Reveal with Restraint" through "Expose With Accountability."
- *Key takeaway:* Marketing can dramatize how the enterprise handles agent truth-telling, building internal and external brand trust as a competitive differentiator.

Chapter 7

Adoption, Scale, and User-Centricity

Scaling AI agents across an enterprise is not a linear march from concept to ubiquity; it is a deliberate choreography. Too many organizations treat adoption as a one-step leap, expecting a good pilot to naturally grow into enterprise scale. History tells us otherwise: the majority of promising AI initiatives stall in the "valley of almost," where political hesitation, resource gaps, and operational bottlenecks grind momentum to a halt. This chapter dismantles that misconception by presenting three principles designed to make adoption sticky. Principle 41: "Small to Scale" begins the sequence by focusing on a narrow, high-impact starting point that is tight enough to manage risk, visible enough to build credibility. From there, Principle 42: "Pilot to Persuade" shifts the focus from mere proof to persuasion, leveraging early wins as organizational currency to defeat skepticism and secure broader commitment. Finally, the newly reframed Principle 43: "Acquire to Amplify" accelerates scaling beyond the limits of organic growth by using targeted acquisitions in technology, talent, or data infrastructure to remove bottlenecks and create exponential deployment velocity.

These principles are not independent suggestions; they are interdependent levers. The narrow start without persuasive evidence dies in obscurity. The persuasive pilot, lacking acquisition muscle, fades under the weight of legacy constraints. Acquisition without early credibility invites political resistance and uncontrolled spending. Focus, persuade, and acquire form the triad and are the three sequential steps that, when executed in sequence, allow scaling to move from aspiration to competitive advantage. Adoption at scale is not a reward for innovation; it is the prize for disciplined sequencing. This chapter will show you how to stage that sequence with precision, giving your AI agents the momentum to leap from isolated pilots to enterprise platforms before your competitors realize you've already won.

DOI: 10.4324/9781003749899-13

Principle 41: Small to Scale

Definition: Start narrow, scale strategically.

"Small to Scale" is the deliberate choice to launch an agent against a single, high-salience use case with clear boundaries, fast feedback, and measurable outcomes, then convert that focused win into a repeatable pattern. Small is not timid; small is surgical. The principle rejects sprawling scope, diffuse metrics, and committee-built designs that try to please every stakeholder on day one. Instead, it asks four questions up front:

1. What micro-workflow will produce undeniable value within a quarter?
2. What outcomes are already on an executive scorecard, making the win legible?
3. What constraints (risk, privacy, legacy systems) must be respected so approval is fast?
4. If this works, where is the next identical sore we can treat with minimal rework?

The narrow start creates three advantages. You can control variance (fewer edge cases), shorten learning loops (weeks, not quarters), and stage a credible moment where the sponsor can claim a business result without apologies. The artifact of success is not a long report; it is a crisp, before-and-after delta tagged to a KPI that leaders already track. The second act is designed in parallel: documentation, templates, rollout kits, and guardrails are prepared while the first use case proves itself. "Scale strategically" means you do not broaden indiscriminately. You expand sideways to similar problems (with comparable data, decisions, and controls) where the cure travels with minimal change. Only after a cluster of identical wins do you attempt a new class of problem. This disciplined replication creates an adoption rhythm the enterprise can absorb: fewer surprises, consistent returns, and a story sponsors can retell without qualification.

Why It Matters to Corporations: Enterprises reward reliability over rhetoric. A narrow initial scope transforms AI from an idea into an instrument by aligning with the decision-making processes of big companies.

- **Budget Traction:** Capital committees approve measures that reduce the plan's risk. A tight use case with audited baselines, holdouts, and pre-agreed outcomes is easy to fund and easy to extend. The CFO sees a unit of ROI they can replicate. The narrative shifts to, "We did X here; we will do X in five more places," rather than "Trust us; the platform will pay off eventually."
- **Risk Posture:** Risk leaders do not resist value; they resist ambiguity. A narrow scope shrinks attack surfaces and clarifies guardrails. You can pre-write the controls memo (purpose limitation, role-based access, reversibility), attach it to the pilot charter, and earn an explicit "yes" that becomes a shield for scaling.
- **Political Momentum:** Behavioral science tells us the peak-end rule shapes memory: people remember the best moment and the ending. A focused launch

creates a strong peak (the visible win) and a clean end (the executive decision to replicate). The social proof then travels: managers reference concrete numbers, not abstractions. Scarcity also works in your favor. Limited early seats create pull from adjacent teams.

- **Engineering Reality:** A narrow scope exposes the real bottlenecks: data hygiene, decision rights, and exception handling, without boiling the ocean. Learning loops improve precision where it counts, and your "release train" rhythm stabilizes. By the time you expand, your telemetry, evaluation suite, and rollback patterns are proven.
- **Organizational Capacity:** Change absorption is finite. Asking one cohort to change a small piece of their day is credible; asking five functions to change everything at once triggers avoidance. Commitment/consistency bias then works in your favor: once a team publicly reports gains from a small change, they are more likely to back the next one.

"Small to Scale" is not a small ambition. It is sequenced ambition. You aim for compounding returns: the second, third, and fourth deployments move faster because you are repeating the cure, not reinventing it. "We limited the first release to five invoice types and one region. It felt conservative until we had 12 weeks of proof and a waiting list." – SVP Finance Transformation, FTSE-100 retailer. Over time, leadership sees a predictable slope: each new site/line/region delivers similar deltas on similar timelines with fewer surprises. The budget shifts from innovation to operations, and the program becomes infrastructure.

Real-World Example: A North American specialty insurer bled margin on mid-value subrogation claims that were too small for attorney escalation and too complex for quick close. The AI team proposed a subrogation agent, but earlier broad claims experiments had eroded trust. They invoked "Small to Scale."

- **Scope:** Auto claims between $5k–$20k, three jurisdictions, two document types.
- **Outcomes:** Recovery rate, cycle time, attorney referral rate, and net cost-to-serve.
- **Controls:** Document redaction by default, human final signatures, and weekly risk reviews.

Within eight weeks, the agent assembled evidence packs overnight, prioritized likely recovery, and drafted the first outreach. Adjusters presented and closed; the agent stayed backstage. Results: recovery rate +17%, cycle time −31%, attorney referrals −22%. The CFO green-lit expansion, but not to "all claims." The team replicated the marine cargo subrogation with the same shape (structured evidence, standardized counterparties, similar controls). Gains were within two points of the first cohort. A third replication in the property matched the pattern again. By quarter's end, the insurer had three identical wins, five executive references, and a backlog of lines asking to be next. The success came not from platform speeches, but from a narrow start with a designed path to scale. The enterprise does not need bigger promises; it needs repeatable proof. "Small to Scale" produces that proof on a cadence that leaders can defend. To institutionalize:

- Write the one-pager before the first line of code: scope, outcomes, guardrails, replication plan.
- Instrument baselines credibly holdouts where possible, clear date windows, and confound notes.
- Build the rollout kit in parallel: templates, controls packet, comms script, and training micro-modules.
- Replicate sideways to same-shape problems first; only later graduate to new classes.
- Publish the cluster: three identical wins form the narrative that unlocks operating funding.

You will be tempted to widen the scope as enthusiasm grows. Resist. Keep the early flywheel tight until your improvement, control, and communications muscles mature. Then scale with speed that looks effortless because it is rehearsed. That is how "pilot" becomes "program" and "program" becomes "how we work."

Principle 42: Pilot to Persuade

Definition: Use pilot performance to defeat skepticism.

A pilot is not a science project; it is a persuasion device. "Pilot to Persuade" designs the scope of every element, measure, audience, and theater to convert neutral or skeptical stakeholders into sponsors. The goal is not merely to "learn"; it is to win the decision to fund, adopt, and extend. There are four design moves to anchor the principle:

1. **Choose the Room:** Who must witness the win for it to matter? Identify the sponsor, the gatekeeper, and the narrator, and align them within the same timeline.
2. **Stage the Metric:** Pick one KPI that the sponsor already reports. No vanity metrics. No new dashboards.
3. **Control the Risk:** Pre-wire risk and compliance with the controls packet; rehearse the fallback. Nothing derails persuasion like a surprise.
4. **Script the Moment:** Build the 12-minute demonstration around a live or recent case that shows the before/after delta. The "peak" must be unmistakable and safe.

Data collection and learning still matter, but they are organized to support decision-making. You plan the story of causality: baselines captured, confounds logged, holdouts used where feasible. You decide in advance how the pilot will end, even if the results are mixed, so the narrative is not hijacked by anecdote. When done, you do not "extend the pilot"; you either scale or stop. Ambiguity is the enemy of persuasion.

Why It Matters to Corporations: Pilots accumulate mythology inside big companies. Many are endless, poorly scoped, or measured on irrelevant proxies. The result is pilot fatigue and learned skepticism: "We tried AI; it did not land." This principle resets the purpose.

- **Political Calculus:** In enterprise settings, belief precedes budget. A well-staged pilot translates technical possibility into executive conviction by giving leaders a win they can speak to succinctly, safely, and in their language. The availability heuristic then works for you: the vivid pilot becomes the mental shortcut leaders use to judge the whole program.
- **Risk Credibility:** When risk leaders co-author the controls and watch them work in the pilot, their endorsement ceases to be a formality. They become narrators of safety, not just reviewers. The messenger effect amplifies persuasion: a message from the CRO carries farther than one from the program team.
- **Frontline Trust:** People do not adopt because a memo says so; they adopt because a respected peer says, "This helped me yesterday." A pilot designed with frontline co-design, dignity-preserving workflows, and human-centered recognition produces defenders who laterally spread usage.
- **Economic Clarity:** Pilots that tie directly to cost-to-serve, revenue protection, or cycle time produce clean ROI math. Finance leaders prefer bounded experiments over broad promises; they can fund the next step with confidence when the evidence is crisp and the exposure contained.
- **Scarcity and Commitment:** Limit early seats. Require a named leader, a risk partner, and a frontline champion to join. Scarcity increases pull; commitment increases follow-through. Structured commitments and visible social proof change behavior faster than generic calls to action.

Pilots fail to persuade when they chase breadth over sharpness, speak to the wrong metric, or let the moment drift. The principal's discipline makes the pilot a decision accelerator: a memorable event, a concise pack to forward, and a signed memo that moves funds and people. "The pilot de-risked the decision in 15 minutes. We saw the delta on our own KPI, and the fallback button worked in real time." – Chief Commercial Officer, global carrier.

Real-World Example: A multinational retailer considered an assortment-planning agent but faced skepticism from Merchandising: "We know our categories." The team proposed a persuasion pilot for seasonal footwear in one region.

- **Room:** EVP Merchandising (sponsor), Chief Risk Officer (gate), two regional GMs (narrators), head of Stores (frontline voice).
- **Metric**: Gross margin dollars in season, plus sell-through at week 6.
- **Controls:** Policy-aligned data only; human override on final assortment; weekly guardrail checks. The pilot ran for eight weeks. The staged moment came in week four: a side-by-side view of two comparable stores, one agent-assisted and one control, showing real sell-through curves and margin dollars.
- **Script the Moment:** The CRO narrated the control story; the GM described staffing relief in allocation. The peak was clean and human. Outcome: +280 bps gross margin in the test stores, 13% faster size-run balance, no increase in markdowns. The EVP approved a phased scale to three adjacent categories and two additional regions. The story that traveled internally was not "AI beat merchants"; it was "the team used the agent to see four weeks forward." That phrasing mattered politically, and the pilot had scripted it.

Persuasion is a design choice. Treating the pilot as a decision instrument, not a sandbox, changes how you plan, run, and close it. To embed the principle:

- Name the decision. Who must say "go," by when, under what evidence? Write it.
- Design the peak. Pick the case and the minute when the audience will feel the delta.
- Co-author safety. Put risk on stage; let them narrate controls.
- Keep it scarce, limited seats, and explicit criteria. Scarcity increases perceived value.
- Close cleanly. Scale or stop. No endless "extensions."

Skepticism is not your enemy; vagueness is. When the pilot shows a sponsor's metric moving, with risk vouching for safety and a respected operator confirming the experience, you collapse months of hesitation into minutes of decision. That is persuasion worthy of capital.

Principle 43: Acquire to Amplify

Definition: Strategic procurement as the catalyst for scalable ai.

Time is leverage when accelerating adoption at scale.

"Acquire to Amplify" is the deliberate use of targeted, strategic acquisitions, whether of technology platforms, niche AI providers, data assets, or specialized talent, to accelerate adoption and scale without reinventing the wheel. It is not about buying for the sake of ownership; it is about integrating capabilities that directly shorten the path from proof of value to enterprise-wide deployment. Time is leverage when accelerating adoption at scale. Internal builds may be slow and politically fraught; starting from scratch can erode first-mover advantage. The acquisition strategy here is surgical:

- Acquire the missing accelerant: a platform, API, dataset, or team that fills a scaling bottleneck.
- Integrate without breaking flow to ensure the new capability seamlessly integrates into the existing tech stack, workflows, and controls.
- Preserve the advantage by building governance, guardrails, and proprietary extensions around the acquired capability to keep it defensible.

A strategic acquisition is judged on time-to-scale, not just ROI. You ask, *Will this make it faster, cheaper, and safer to deploy agents across multiple use cases?* If the answer is yes, you align capital allocation, procurement velocity, and integration playbooks to strike fast. The principle also demands future-proofing. A hurried acquisition that creates future tech debt is a liability. "Acquire to Amplify" means you evaluate whether the target accelerates today's scaling goals and supports your multi-year AI roadmap.

Why It Matters to Corporations: In enterprise AI, scaling is often blocked not by imagination but by infrastructure gaps. These gaps may include:

- Missing model orchestration layers.
- Insufficient labeled datasets for niche domains.
- Lack of specialized compliance tooling.
- Scarcity of high-skill AI engineering talent.

Each gap becomes a brake on adoption speed. Strategic acquisitions remove these brakes in one decisive move, transforming the adoption curve from a linear crawl to an exponential ramp.

- **Speed to Market:** When competitors are in the same experimentation phase, the first to scale proven pilots into full production often wins the customer loyalty, data flywheel, and market perception game. Acquiring a ready-made capability, especially one proven in a comparable enterprise environment, removes 6–18 months of internal build time.
- **Risk Management:** A well-chosen acquisition can de-risk scaling by importing already-certified, regulator-approved components into your tech stack. This is particularly valuable where regulatory clearance is a significant barrier, as it is in banking, health care, and defense.

- **Economic Efficiency:** Building from scratch burns engineering cycles and opportunity costs. Buying strategically compresses the cost curve by considering faster adoption, earlier revenue protection, and a reduced support burden from a more mature solution.
- **Talent Concentration:** Acquiring AI talent, particularly those who have already solved adjacent scaling problems, injects institutional memory and deployment discipline that cannot be trained overnight.
- **Defensive Positioning:** Owning the scaling accelerant makes it harder for competitors to follow your exact adoption pattern. For example, suppose you acquire the best compliance-monitoring module for LLM agents in your sector. In that case, you can embed it into every deployment, making your adoption both faster and safer, and giving you a harder-to-replicate advantage.

This principle also recognizes the political capital inherent in acquisition. When executives see a tangible, external investment tied to adoption, it signals seriousness and urgency. It reframes AI scaling from "IT initiative" to "corporate growth mandate."

Real-World Example: A Tier-1 global bank piloted an AI agent to automate structured credit risk assessments. The pilot was a success, achieving a 20% faster turnaround and 9% fewer post-close compliance flags, but scaling stalled. The blocker: the risk-monitoring pipeline required manual exception handling across multiple jurisdictions. Rather than building the exception-handling module internally, the bank acquired a fintech specializing in multi-jurisdiction regulatory compliance for automated decision systems. The fintech's platform is already integrated with 14 regulatory data sources and has been certified by multiple EU regulators. Within four months, the acquired capability was integrated into the risk agent workflow. This eliminated the main scaling barrier, enabling the bank to deploy the agent to seven additional jurisdictions in less than 12 months. Key results include the scaling timeline was reduced by 15 months compared to the internal build estimate; deployment costs per jurisdiction decreased by 42%; and the regulatory approval cycle time was halved. The acquisition was not about owning a fintech for prestige, but rather about acquiring the scaling enabler. By targeting the exact capability that was slowing rollout, the bank shifted from a single-country pilot to a global deployment within the fiscal year. Scaling AI is a race against both competitors and organizational entropy. Internal builds alone rarely win that race; the bureaucracy, talent constraints, and shifting priorities inside large corporations are too slow.

"Acquire to Amplify" addresses this by treating strategic acquisition as an adoption lever rather than a side activity of corporate development. Acquisition here is not the end; it is the acceleration point. It is about taking a proven pilot and turning it into an enterprise-wide norm before the market moves on. The best practice sequence is shown in Figure 7.1.

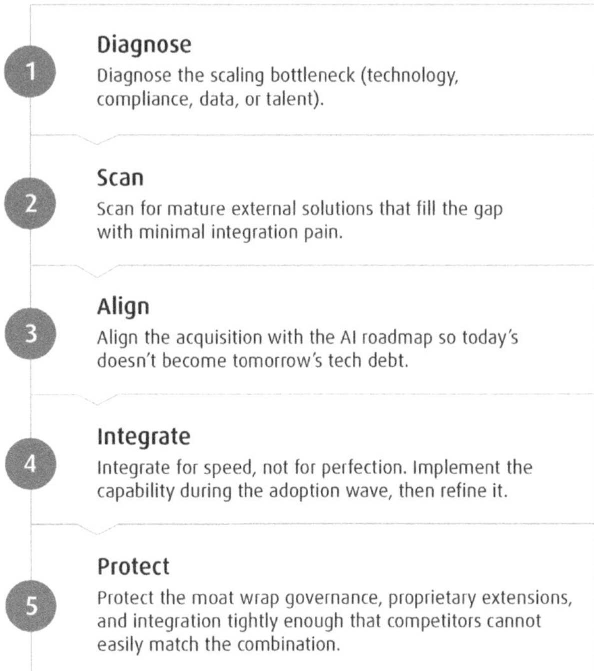

Figure 7.1 "Acquire to Amplify" best practice sequence to accelerate an acquisition from a proven pilot to enterprise-wide norm. Diagram by BMO Financial Group.

Chapter 7 Conclusion: The Scaling Triad From Narrow Wins to Enterprise Dominance

Adoption and scaling depend on intentional design. Many organizations incorrectly treat a successful pilot as the endpoint, when in fact it's just the ignition spark. Leaders must orchestrate deliberate steps to enable broader adoption. The process starts with a tightly focused, strategically chosen pilot that establishes control, credibility, and measurable outcomes. This controlled success serves as compelling evidence, allowing leaders to win over skeptics and secure commitment from the wider organization. Then the "Acquire to Amplify" approach accelerates growth. At this stage, targeted acquisitions transform linear growth into exponential growth. Securing core infrastructure, compliance resources, or talent isn't optional; it's like lifting a speed limiter from a racecar. Skipping this step stalls progress, drains momentum, and allows competitors to catch up. The resulting scaling flywheel is win early with focus, use those wins to persuade, and amplify adoption by removing friction through strategic acquisition. Repeat this sequence across different functions, markets, or geographies, and your AI adoption becomes not just possible, but unstoppable.

The lesson of this chapter is discipline. Leaders cannot view scale as a one-time event. It is a rhythm: pilot, persuade, expand, repeat. Each cycle builds momentum. Each stage enhances credibility. By starting small, persuading intentionally, and scaling strategically, growth becomes viable. The danger is impatience. Executives, under pressure from boards and markets, often want scale now. They announce prematurely, triggering backlash. They skip persuasion, generating resistance. They ignore procurement, wasting time and capital reinventing. Impatience destroys adoption, whereas discipline sustains it. Ultimately, scaling is about the narrative and not just the technology. It is the story of how small victories become large ones, how pilots become proof points, how procurement becomes acceleration. The organizations that scale smart will not be those that shout loudest. They will be those who earned it, step by step, through credibility, persuasion, and user trust.

Persona Highlights

Jordan, Chief Strategy & Transformation Officer

- Anchors on "Small to Scale" and "Pilot to Persuade."
- *Key takeaway:* Scaling is a sequence of wins, each designed to persuade the board and prove credibility for the next stage.

Claire, Chief Financial Officer

- Resonates with "Pilot to Persuade" and "Acquire to Amplify."
- *Key takeaway:* Pilots must produce quantifiable ROI, and acquisitions can accelerate returns faster than organic builds.

Rafael, Chief Technology Officer

- Values "Acquire to Amplify."
- *Key takeaway:* Procurement is a strategic lever; partnerships and acquisitions can scale adoption faster than internal development alone.

Simone, Chief Human Resources Officer

- Sees "Small to Scale" as a workforce imperative.
- *Key takeaway:* Incremental adoption reduces fear, builds employee trust, and prevents cultural backlash.

Mo, Chief Marketing Officer

- Energized by "Pilot to Persuade."
- *Key takeaway:* Pilots should be staged as persuasive theater, transforming wins into narratives that build momentum internally and enhance brand leadership externally.

Part III Conclusion

The final stage of intelligence is rhythm. Enterprises that succeed at scale follow a disciplined cycle: prove, persuade, expand, then govern. Each victory creates social proof, which gradually hardens into a formal process. By standardizing adoption metrics, managing Human:Agent ratios, and ensuring transparency, organizations transform bursts of innovation into solid infrastructure. Success shifts from being occasional to becoming predictable. When trust, transparency, and adaptability intersect, enterprises stop pursuing transformation; instead, they accelerate it. Tomorrow's leaders won't simply deploy agents, they'll architect the operating systems for enterprise intelligence. Their legacy will be a maturity model for others to follow, not just a collection of pilots or platforms. Value is measured in confidence gained and intelligence amplified, rather than mere cost savings or automation.

DOI: 10.4324/9781003749899-14

Conclusion

The New Seat of Influence

Chapter 8

From Deployment to Doctrine

Executives can boil this down into a 10-Move Enterprise Playbook, a framework for disciplined execution. Each move stems from the 43 principles governing the development of AI agents within the enterprise, forming a deliberate sequence of actions that, when executed with discipline, provide a strategic advantage. These ten moves illustrate an often-overlooked principle: AI success hinges not just on speed, but also on direction, precision, and governance. Sequenced like dominoes, each move activates the next, constructing a disciplined framework for execution. This structure shields the enterprise from hype, protects against failure, and ensures readiness for scalable transformation. Accordingly, leadership must transition from merely chasing new technology to strategically architecting the enterprise's next operating system. The reward is market leadership, not just marginal efficiency.

AI success hinges not just on speed, but also on direction, precision, and governance.

The 10-Move Enterprise Playbook for AI Agents lays out a structured pathway for corporate leaders aiming to move from experimentation to scaled execution. Each move recognizes that AI agents are not just peripheral tools but strategic enablers of enterprise intelligence. The framework emphasizes that adoption is not achieved through rhetoric but through disciplined alignment of technology, economics, leadership, and trust. In the modern corporate landscape, adopting artificial intelligence is no longer just a speculative venture or a luxury reserved for the technologically daring. Adopting artificial intelligence has become

DOI: 10.4324/9781003749899-16

Table 8.1 Ten-Move Enterprise Playbook for AI Agents. Diagram by BMO Financial Group.

Strategic Move	*Description*
1. Anchor Deployment to Business Goals	The first imperative is strategic alignment. Agents must never be justified by novelty or innovative theater. Their role is to deliver measurable outcomes, whether in cost containment, compliance efficiency, or top-line growth. This grounding secures boardroom support and ensures sustained capital allocation.
2. Define the End State Before You Code	Strategic execution begins with clarity of conclusion. Leaders must articulate the target operating model and reverse-engineer design decisions accordingly. This prevents wasted investment, misaligned builds, and the slow erosion of credibility.
3. Launch Quietly, Execute Boldly	Premature fanfare is dangerous. By announcing too soon, organizations arouse scrutiny, skepticism, and internal politics that can derail momentum. Silent launches with decisive execution protect the enterprise and allow results to speak for themselves.
4. Sequence With Discipline, Scale in Stages	Timing is decisive. Rollouts must align with organizational readiness, beginning with business units capable of absorbing change. Scaling must be incremental, with governance frameworks preventing chaos. This balances ambition with discipline.
5. Engineer for Craveability and Trust	Adoption cannot be mandated; it must be earned. Agents must be intuitive, integrated, and trustworthy. The first agent functions as a showpiece proof that the enterprise is serious, competent, and credible. Design principles must emphasize zero-learning curves and invisible integration into workflows.
6. Demand Economic Justification	The enterprise cannot indulge in costless innovation. Every agent must be grounded in economic value. Processes should be optimized before automation, ROI must be quantified, and the Human:Agent ratio should be governed as a board-level metric. Economic proof is the currency of adoption.
7. Secure Political Capital Early	Adoption is not only economic; it is political. Agents succeed when they align with leadership agendas. Executives must map power structures, win over functional leaders, and stage symbolic wins to build momentum. Without political capital, technical victories dissolve into organizational resistance.

(*Continued*)

Table 8.1 (Continued)

8. Recode the Operating Model	Incremental layering will not suffice. To capture true advantage, enterprises must redesign their operating model around agent-first principles. This requires introducing new roles, institutionalizing learning loops, and embedding adaptability into organizational DNA.
9. Govern Trust Through Restraint	Transparency must be selective. Agents should not drown stakeholders in explanations; outcomes must speak louder than outputs. Limitations must be disclosed before failure, and truths surfaced with accountability. Trust, once earned, becomes the multiplier of adoption.
10. Scale by Proof, Not Proclamation	The final move demands humility in scaling. Adoption must be earned through pilots that persuade skeptics, procurement strategies that accelerate capability, and expansions that validate credibility. Grand declarations without proof risk enterprise reputation; scaling through evidence builds unassailable trust.

essential for competitiveness. For financial services, health care, manufacturing, and other industries facing structural transformation, the rise of AI agents is not simply another chapter in automation. It marks a crucial shift toward enterprise intelligence. The question is no longer whether to embrace agents, but how to do so with discipline, foresight, and authority. What sets successful adopters apart from those who falter is not access to technology; everyone can acquire cloud computing, algorithmic power, and vendor solutions right-sized for the scale of their operation (big or small). The key difference is deliberate, sequenced execution. Companies that execute with rigor transform not just workflows but entire operating models, unlocking measurable economics, strategic influence, and lasting trust.

These ten moves are not isolated steps. They are a practical extension of the 43 principles, designed to guide real-world execution. When applied with discipline, they help turn strategic intent into measurable progress.

The Architecture of Disciplined Execution

Together, these ten moves embody an operating philosophy and methodology. They provide a disciplined path forward: start with strategy, anchor in economics, secure leadership buy-in, design for adoption, embed trust, and scale through evidence. For boards and executives, the implications are significant. Rolling out

AI agents is not a question of if, but of how. Organizations that fail to act decisively will find themselves lagging behind competitors who are already codifying the Human:Agent ratio, embedding agents into their operating models, and staging wins that shift market narratives. The time for experimental theater has ended. The time for disciplined execution has begun. The enterprise that adopts this playbook will not only deploy AI agents but also redefine itself as an intelligent, adaptive, and strategically aligned organization. In doing so, it will convert technology into influence and influence into advantage. That is the essence of the 10-Move Enterprise Playbook: not automation for its own sake, but orchestration for competitive leadership.

Chapter 9

What Leaders Must Understand About the Technical Core

Every era of transformation produces a new form of illiteracy. During the Industrial Revolution, financial illiteracy was a significant issue; leaders who could not read balance sheets lost their firms. In the digital age, data illiteracy led executives who failed to understand information flows to cede competitive ground. In the age of AI agents, the new illiteracy is technical illiteracy in governance. The paradox of progress is that strategy is now inseparable from technical architecture. Executives cannot meaningfully govern what they cannot conceptually grasp. Strategic authority depends on informed curiosity. This chapter closes the final gap in this book's argument: the one between vision and execution, between boardroom strategy and system architecture. It is not a technical manual; it is a fluency guide for leaders who must understand the machinery of the future without becoming engineers. The goal is not to code, but to comprehend. To know just enough to interrogate wisely, govern confidently, and prevent the most dangerous phrase in corporate transformation: "I didn't know how it worked."

Understanding the Data

Data is to AI what capital is to finance. It is the foundational asset that underwrites every decision, forecast, and prediction. Yet most organizations still treat data as plumbing rather than policy. For leaders, the first shift in mindset is this: data architecture is strategy made visible. It reveals how decisions flow, how accountability is structured, and how value is created. Executives must grasp five architectural truths:

1. **Data Lineage:** Every dataset has a life story – origin, movement, and transformation. Lineage tracking ensures auditability, which is vital in regulated sectors such as banking, health care, and energy. It enables leaders to answer questions regulators increasingly ask: Where did this insight come from? What transformations occurred? Who authorized it? Without lineage, explainability collapses.

DOI: 10.4324/9781003749899-17

2. **Data Quality:** Models amplify the quality of their inputs. Garbage in still means garbage multiplied. Executives should understand how quality is measured: through completeness, accuracy, consistency, and timeliness. Sophisticated organizations now use data observability platforms that automatically flag anomalies and latency issues – concepts leaders must know well enough to demand.
3. **Interoperability and Integration:** The technical term hides a strategic truth – interoperability is a proxy for collaboration. When systems can't talk to each other, neither can teams. Leaders should push for open standards (like RESTful APIs and cloud-native data fabrics) and support metadata catalogs that unify the organization's semantic layer. This turns data into a shared language across business functions.
4. **Governance Frameworks:** Beyond access rights, governance now includes data ethics, bias management, and privacy engineering. Executives should insist that every data asset has an owner, every dataset has a quality SLA, and every use case is logged for compliance. Governance without accountability is theater.
5. **Data as Capital:** The most forward-thinking firms quantify the ROI of clean data. They use metrics such as "data downtime reduction," "trust scores," or "time-to-insight." By treating data as balance-sheet capital rather than technical cost, leaders elevate architecture to strategy.

When the C-suite frames data as an enterprise asset, architecture becomes a corporate narrative. Clean data signals discipline. Fragmented data exposes dysfunction. The architecture of information becomes the architecture of trust.

From Models to Agents: Translating Complexity Into Governance

AI agents are not traditional software but are living systems. They perceive, interpret, decide, and act, often in stochastic (probabilistic) ways that make conventional deterministic governance obsolete. To lead confidently, executives must understand the conceptual anatomy of AI systems and how each layer interacts with accountability.

The Agent Stack

- **Foundation Models:** These are large-scale neural networks pretrained on vast datasets (e.g., GPT, Claude, Gemini). They provide linguistic or perceptual intelligence but must be fine-tuned or prompt-engineered for enterprise use. Leaders must grasp the trade-offs: proprietary models offer control but demand capital; open models offer speed but increase risk exposure.

- **Prompt and Context Layers:** Agents rely on context windows and retrieval-augmented generation (RAG) to ground answers in enterprise data. Understanding these concepts helps leaders assess hallucination risk. A CEO need not code the RAG pipeline, but should ask: *How is corporate data retrieved, ranked, and verified before the model responds?*
- **Decision Logic and Workflow Orchestration:** Beneath the conversational interface lies the logic layer: rules, APIs, and triggers that execute actions (like generating reports or approving transactions). Errors here can cause operational havoc. Governance requires audit trails and human-in-the-loop checkpoints.
- **Guardrails and Ethics Engines:** Modern agents include policy layers that filter responses, block unsafe actions, or escalate anomalies. Leaders should ensure these filters align with corporate risk appetite and regulatory standards, not just vendor defaults.
- **Monitoring and Retraining:** Models drift. Over time, accuracy decays as the world changes. Leaders should understand model drift detection, retraining pipelines, and machine learning operations (MLOps). MLOps is the operational discipline that keeps models current. A well-governed enterprise mandates retraining frequency with the same rigor as financial reporting cycles.

Integration and Adaptability: From Pilots to Enterprise Systems

The most complex technical challenge with AI agents is not building – it is *scaling*. Pilots are controlled ecosystems; enterprises are chaotic organisms. Integration is where governance meets reality. Leaders should recognize that scaling requires systemic interoperability across three planes:

1. **Data Plane:** Where the agent connects to data lakes, APIs, or transactional systems. Poorly designed integrations lead to latency, duplication, and exposure of sensitive information. Leaders must insist on encryption at rest and in transit, role-based access control, and compliance with data-residency regulations (e.g., GDPR, PIPEDA).
2. **Application Plane:** Where the agent interfaces with existing platforms like CRM, ERP, and Human Resource Information System (HRIS) systems. Here, API versioning and middleware orchestration become strategic topics. Enterprises that neglect middleware soon drown in incompatible interfaces.
3. **Experience Plane:** The human interface layer. Agents succeed when users experience effortless interaction integrated into tools they already use (Slack, Outlook, Teams). Adoption depends on invisibility. A technically elegant but behaviorally disruptive agent will fail.

As integration deepens, attack surfaces expand. Leaders must understand zero-trust architecture, identity federation, and anomaly detection. Cybersecurity is not a separate discipline; it is the immune system of integration. Equally vital is compliance automation, embedding audit logs and explainability into every agent action. Regulators are beginning to demand AI traceability reports showing inputs, decisions, and outcomes. Leaders who pre-empt these expectations protect enterprise reputation.

Scalable integration demands operational adaptability. Agents must evolve as business logic, regulations, and market conditions shift. Technically, this means building modular architectures, such as microservices, that can be swapped out without rewriting the entire stack. Strategically, it means budgeting for continuous improvement, not one-time launches. Executives should familiarize themselves with MLOps and AIOps (AI for IT operations). These frameworks automate model deployment, monitoring, and incident response. Knowing their vocabulary allows leaders to interrogate reliability metrics: *How fast can we retrain after drift? What is our mean time to recovery (MTTR)?* Ultimately, adaptability is a condition of survival. The only constant in AI is change, and so systems that cannot flex will fracture. Leaders who understand the mechanics of integration will turn scale from fragility into strategic resilience.

The only constant in AI is change, and so systems that cannot flex will fracture.

Governance cannot be outsourced to technologists or consultants; it must be owned by leadership. The distance between understanding and authority is shrinking fast. To lead in this era, executives must cultivate informed curiosity, the willingness to probe beyond dashboards, to challenge assumptions, to see technology not as magic but as a mechanism. They must know enough to ask why a model behaves as it does, how a dataset flows through the organization, and where an agent makes decisions without human eyes. This does not mean every leader must become a data scientist. But every leader must become technically bilingual, able to converse fluently in the grammar of governance and the syntax of systems. Strategy is no longer just about market positioning; it is about data integrity, model reliability, and architectural resilience. Executives don't need the math; they need the mechanics of accountability. Here are some example questions that anchor governance discipline:

- *Where does human oversight begin and end?*
- *Which decisions are autonomous, and which require escalation?*

- *What failsafe exists if an agent's judgment contradicts policy?*
- *How is bias tested across protected classes or geographies?*
- *What logs prove compliance when regulators inquire?*

These questions transform governance from abstraction to structure. They make invisible systems visible to the board. Finally, leaders must internalize the cultural truth: AI governance is not about limiting intelligence; it is about protecting legitimacy. Every misstep by an agent is a trust event, and trust is a balance sheet entry. Leaders who comprehend how models behave, learn, and fail are the only ones equipped to govern their consequences.

AI governance is not about limiting intelligence; it is about protecting legitimacy.

The organizations that thrive will be those whose leaders treat comprehension as a form of control. They will invest in executive education on AI fluency, build cross-functional governance boards, and integrate technical KPIs into performance scorecards. They will view architecture reviews as strategic rituals, not compliance chores. The gap between strategy and implementation is not a technical gap; it is a leadership one. The leaders who bridge this gap will define the next generation of enterprise intelligence. They will not just deploy agents; they will govern ecosystems. And in doing so, they will ensure that AI serves not as an external force of disruption, but as an internal instrument of design.

Conclusion

From Experiment to Infrastructure

It was once sufficient to compete by leveraging efficiency, digitization, and automation. Now, these are table stakes, and the precision of artificial intelligence is what is needed to differentiate and compete. The 43 principles in *Return on Intelligence* redefine how AI agents succeed inside complex institutions. This body of work is a transformation, a disciplined approach to converting technological potential into institutional permanence. The transformation is expressed in the capacity to influence decisions, orchestrate resources, shift behavior, and establish permanence. AI agents will not secure their place within the enterprise solely because of their novelty, nor will they succeed simply because of technical sophistication. The Concorde supersonic jet, Google Glass, and the Segway are examples of superior technologies that each failed to be generally adopted. The difference in an AI agent's success and adoption will be whether it can secure legitimacy through economics, narrative, political alignment, and behavioral reinforcement. *Return on Intelligence* positions AI agents as instruments of enterprise influence via a framework that anchors on shaping perception, reconfiguring workflows, and altering decision-making structures. They should be deployed with a bold, unified strategy to unlock an enduring capability.

The Subtle Arrival of Transformation

Transformation rarely arrives with sudden spectacle. Transformation begins small, maybe in a conference room, with a couple of dry-erase markers and a whiteboard. With dedicated, motivated leadership, transformation gradually permeates existing processes until it becomes routine. This is precisely how AI agents will transform organizations: they will first appear in pilots and small, strategic initiatives, where inefficiencies and indifference coexist. AI will take on tasks that humans have long avoided, such as data reconciliation, service triage, and compliance interpretation, executing them efficiently without the fatigue or emotions of a human. As their reliability compounds, they will expose

DOI: 10.4324/9781003749899-18

operational fragility that leadership once tolerated as "just the cost of doing business." Gradually, agents will migrate from the periphery to the core. Decision flows that are too trivial for human review but too numerous for scale will become their domain. In doing so, they will alter the rhythms of work. Meetings shorten, cycle times compress, and judgment migrates closer to the edge of data. What started as an experiment will, over time, evolve into critical infrastructure. Initially, organizations may see an agent as a tool or supplement. But as agents prove reliable, trust will deepen, dependencies will grow, and resistance will fade. One day, leaders will look back and realize that what began as a trial has quietly become a necessity. That is the true hallmark of transformation: it does not demand attention; it achieves permanence. The structural disciplines of the 43 principles in this playbook determine whether AI agents achieve permanence or perish as experiments and coalesce into four governing dimensions:

1. **Strategic Deployment:** Agents must be introduced with discipline, sequenced into receptive parts of the organization, and scaled with intent. They succeed not when they are everywhere, but when they are in the right place, at the right time, solving the correct problems. Strategic deployment resists the temptation of hype and prioritizes readiness over speed.
2. **Political Orchestration:** Influence circulates between leaders, gatekeepers, and frontline actors. Agents succeed when they align with this circuitry. They must reinforce leadership agendas, stage symbolic wins, and secure sponsorship from those who control adoption. Without political orchestration, technical victories collapse under organizational resistance.
3. **Trust Design:** Trust is not a by-product; it is engineered. Agents must be seamless, invisible, and user-friendly. Their outputs must be outcomes, not explanations. Their limits must be disclosed before failure, not after. Trust design builds confidence not through transparency for its own sake, but through selective revelation and reliable performance.
4. **Behavioral Influence:** Adoption is ultimately human. Agents succeed when they alter habits, reduce friction, and offer relief. They must demonstrate effortlessness, expose hidden value, and create emotional buy-in at the frontline. When users want to use them not because they are mandated to, but because they make life easier, agents transition from novelty to necessity.

The Shift From Pilot to Platform

Across industries, the same story is playing out. A team begins with a pilot: a chatbot for compliance queries, an underwriting co-pilot, a call center workflow triage agent. Management has a narrow scope and modest expectations for the pilot initiative, and at first, most seem ok with experimentation. The transformation begins when the pilot is executed in accordance with the principles codified here: anchored to business outcomes, shielded from premature fanfare, designed for trust, and reinforced politically. That same pilot, which started as an idea on a whiteboard, gains momentum. Other teams hear of its benefits, and other leaders start citing it as evidence of AI progress. Adoption grows organically. Within months, what was once an isolated initiative is woven into the daily routines of hundreds of employees. And before long, the agent ceases to be a project and becomes part of the infrastructure. The organization no longer "uses" an agent; it runs on it. This shift is an intentional and predictable result of disciplined deployment, political alignment, trust architecture, and behavioral insights. It is, in short, a consequence of following the principles of AI agents. It exemplifies the *Return on Intelligence* mindset: the ability to turn experimentation into infrastructure and insight into institutional advantage. In this new era, leadership is judged by how effectively both human and machine intelligence are mobilized to achieve scale. Your task is to deploy a powerful strategy that converts technological potential into institutional permanence.

The Future Reframed

Looking ahead a quinquennial, competitive advantage will not belong to the firms with the most advanced models, but to those that have strategically embedded intelligence, through agents or otherwise, into the very fabric of their infrastructure. Market dominance will be defined by institutionalization: intelligence made operational, measurable, and trusted. In this world, two new metrics will matter most. The **Human:Agent ratio** will reveal how efficiently the enterprise converts intelligence into capacity. **Intelligent operating leverage** will expose how effectively that capacity compounds value. Together, they will become the dual indicators of productivity and adaptability in an AI-governed economy. Boardrooms will use agent adoption as a proxy for agility; regulators will judge not only what agents do, but how they are governed, audited, and aligned with fiduciary responsibility. The leaders who endure will be those who master the unseen architecture of this transformation, the choreography of influence, the sequencing of strategic deployment, the orchestration of political capital, and the quiet power of empathy-by-design. The principles are set. The only question that remains is whether you will execute.

Author's Reflection

The Future of Intelligent Architecture

In the first chapters of this book, we explored how intelligence scales within an enterprise and how leaders transition from automation to agency, from data pipelines to decision ecosystems. Yet as we close, the next horizon of innovation reveals itself: a world where intelligence is no longer bound by static code, linear time, or fixed space. The enterprise of the future is being architected through extended context cognition, systems that can see, reason, and act across an entire repository of logic, policy, and purpose. This is not mere automation. It is the evolution of digital stewardship: AI agents that understand the architecture they inhabit. With a million-token context windows and whole-repo comprehension, these systems will refactor themselves as business models shift, embedding compliance, ethics, and design standards not through governance committees but through living code.

We are entering an era of time-varying and space-varying modalities, intelligent systems that adapt continuously to when and where they operate.

At the same time, we are entering an era of time-varying and space-varying modalities, and intelligent systems that continuously adapt to when and where they operate. Market cycles, regulatory regimes, consumer sentiment, and even geopolitical signals all form spatiotemporal fields that require dynamic

DOI: 10.4324/9781003749899-19

calibration. The most successful AI enterprises will design agents that read these fields as naturally as a pilot reads the wind. The static model gives way to the adaptive intelligence system, one that learns not just from history, but also within context, across dimensions, and through time. Beneath this orchestration lies the hardware frontier, the silent revolution of kernel optimization on next-generation accelerators. Here, performance becomes philosophy. The question "How many GPUs do we own?" becomes "How efficiently does intelligence propagate through our architecture?" Optimized kernels, fused operators, and AI-tuned compilers are the new engines of return on intelligence (ROI_2) in the digital age. Together they define how fast insights flow, how sustainably compute scales, and how competitively intelligence compounds.

These three pillars, self-refactoring code, spatiotemporal learning, and hardware-aware intelligence, mark the beginning of a post-static enterprise – an organization where architecture is alive, continuously evolving, and ethically aligned, an organization that no longer treats technology as an enabler, but as a coauthor of leadership. If the first era of AI taught us to automate, the next will teach us to architect dynamically. Intelligence will not just analyze performance; it will become the performance, measured in speed, precision, trust, and adaptability. That is the true return on intelligence: a system that learns as fast as its leaders dream and a leadership culture brave enough to let it. The future will belong to those who master this duality, the human capacity for judgment and the machine's capacity for scale. Together, they form the new organizational DNA: intelligent by design, adaptive by default, and continuously compounding in value.

And that, ultimately, is where this story ends, at the threshold of a new one.

Appendix A

Personas

In enterprise strategy and transformation, personas are a powerful tool for bridging abstract ideas with real-world understanding. A persona is more than a demographic profile; it is a thoughtfully constructed representation of an archetype, such as an executive stakeholder, frontline user, or customer segment. When deploying AI agents, personas clarify whom the agent serves, the friction points it addresses, and the narratives that encourage adoption. By grounding deployments in the real experiences of their intended users and aligning them with desired outcomes, personas help ensure practical and relevant solutions. Below are five personas developed to provide that clarity for the 43 principles within:

- **Jordan, Chief Strategy & Transformation Officer**
- **Claire, Chief Financial Officer**
- **Rafael, Chief Technology Officer**
- **Simone, Chief Human Resources Officer**
- **Mo, Chief Marketing Officer**

Executive Persona – Chief Strategy & Transformation Officer

Name: Jordan Chen
Age: 47
Title: Chief Strategy & Transformation Officer
Company: Global Fortune 500 Bank (NYC HQ)
Education: MBA, Wharton School; BS, Applied Economics, Cornell University
Background: 18+ years in financial services, 10 in enterprise strategy, 4 leading innovation portfolios
Aspiration: To make AI real – visible ROI, operational traction, career-defining wins
Fears: Getting stuck in pilot purgatory, losing credibility with the C-suite, getting outflanked by competitors deploying more innovative systems

Challenges

- Internal resistance to change
- Innovation teams disconnected from revenue outcomes
- Technical teams building without business backing
- C-suite demands to "prove the value of AI"

Jordan needs more than ideas; he needs leverage, social proof, and a narrative to align the boardroom, the frontline, and the back-office.

Strategic Profile

Jordan is a hybrid executive – part operator, part visionary. He thrives in ambiguity, aligning silos and driving transformation. With mounting pressure to scale AI, he's focused on embedding agents into workflows that deliver measurable value. His goal: make AI indispensable, not theoretical.

Motivations

- **Deliver Tangible Value:** Jordan's performance is tied to margin growth, business agility, and innovation that sticks. He has no patience for vanity metrics or AI for AI's sake.
- **Protect Reputation:** He is aware that if his AI agenda fails, it won't be the CTO or the vendor who takes the blame. It'll be him.
- **Shift Power:** Jordan is frustrated by how legacy technology decisions continue to dictate modern strategy. He wants to use agents to reconfigure internal power structures subtly.
- **Become a Builder:** While he is not a technologist by training, Jordan sees himself as a builder of business models, systems, and future-proofed teams.
- **Leave a Legacy:** He does not want a promotion. He aims to be the executive recognized for transforming AI from a concept into a capability that altered the firm's trajectory.

Frustrations

- **Pilot Purgatory:** He has funded 11 pilots in 18 months, and 5 have delivered value. Only one made it past procurement.
- **Technical-First Mindset:** His AI team focuses on models, not on outcomes. Their success metrics do not map to revenue, risk, or readiness.
- **Stakeholder Resistance:** Business units fear agents will take jobs or complicate workflows. Compliance teams want every model to be explainable. Leaders are skeptical unless ROI is instant.

- **Innovation Theater:** He is constantly being pitched futuristic ideas without operational alignment. Everyone's chasing the next big thing; nobody's focused on what ships.

Mental Models

- **Agents Are Coworkers:** Jordan does not see agents as tech. He sees them as digital employees, hired to perform, tracked for impact, and fired if they underdeliver.
- **Narrative Is Leverage:** He understands that no AI tool gets adopted unless it comes with a story that makes adoption feel sticky.
- **Pain Before Possibility:** He does not sell new tech by promising potential. He sells it by framing it as the solution to a visible pain point.
- **Shadow Wins Beat Central Mandates:** He infiltrates departments where allies are present. Let the win surface organically. Then scales.
- **Design for Drift:** He knows the business changes every quarter. He is obsessed with adaptive systems – agents that evolve as the organization shifts.

Five Most Significant Principles to Jordan

1. Principle 1: Business Before Buzz – Tie Agent Deployment to Business Outcomes, Not Innovation Agendas.
2. Principle 2: Outcomes Matter – Design for Business Outcomes.
3. Principle 19: Prove the Return – Every Agent Needs an Economic Justification.
4. Principle 20: Govern the Future – The Human:Agent Ratio Is Not Just a Number; It Is a Corporate Truth Serum.
5. Principle 25: Map the Power – Build Stakeholder Maps Before Agent Design.

Key Messages for Jordan

- This is not about agents; it is about strategy. Every principle translates directly into enterprise value and competitive positioning.
- The Human:Agent ratio is your north star. It operationalizes transformation in a way that boards, regulators, and investors respect.
- Your political capital is on the line. Use principles of buy-in and executive theater to frame wins and sustain momentum.
- Economic justification is non-negotiable. Every agent must tie back to measurable ROI.
- Scale is earned, not announced. Narrow wins when staged correctly become institutional doctrine.

Personalized Chapter Excerpts

Chapter 1 – Strategic Deployment and Execution

Jordan prioritizes business outcomes over innovation theater. Agents must earn credibility through measurable impact.

Chapter 3 – Economic Justification and Return on Investment

Jordan's world is measured in shareholder letters. Frameworks like "Fix First, Then Automate" help turn transformation into economic power.

Governance is essential. The Human:Agent ratio becomes Jordan's steering wheel for linking AI adoption to shareholder outcomes.

Chapter 4 – Leadership, Influence, and Political Buy-In

Coalition building is key. Mapping power and staging wins helps Jordan accelerate adoption across resistant units.

Executive Persona – Chief Financial Officer

Name: Claire DuPont

Age: 55

Title: Chief Financial Officer

Company: Fortune 200 Global Financial Institution

Location: Chicago, IL

Education: MBA, Texas A&M University Mays School of Business; BA, Mathematics & Economics, Stanford University

Background: 30+ years in finance, 14 years in CFO and divisional finance leadership roles across banking, insurance, and asset management

Aspiration: To fund initiatives that deliver measurable ROI, improve financial resilience, and reduce operational variability

Fears: Funding AI without a clear return, compromising auditability, or losing credibility with regulators and shareholders

Challenges

- AI proposals lacking financial rigor
- Pressure to improve operational leverage without increasing headcount
- Rising compliance costs and regulatory complexity
- Unclear ownership and governance of AI initiatives
- Tech budgets are expanding without a proportional impact

Claire needs more than innovative language; she needs financial clarity, risk transparency, and performance accountability.

Strategic Profile

Claire is a disciplined financial leader who demands clarity on ROI and operational resilience. She funds what performs, not what promises. Her mission: deploy agents that deliver measurable margin, reduce risk, and enhance transparency, without compromising auditability or shareholder trust.

Motivations

- **Economic Justification:** Claire's top priority is simple: What is the return? Everything else is noise. She does not oppose innovation; she opposes misaligned investments.
- **Institutional Resilience:** She sees AI as a potential accelerator, but only if it improves auditability, control, and business continuity.
- **Capital Efficiency:** Claire is under constant pressure from shareholders and rating agencies to improve operational leverage. She needs to show productivity gains without adding headcount.
- **Forecasting Accuracy:** She is obsessed with reducing variability in earnings, cost structures, and forecasts. Anything that stabilizes performance earns her attention.
- **Regulatory Clarity:** In a post-SOX, post-Basel world, Claire knows the cost of compliance. If agents can improve transparency, reduce reporting burdens, or enhance control environments, she'll listen.

Frustrations

- **AI Without ROI:** She has sat through too many AI briefings that lead with buzzwords rather than business cases. She does not fund "innovation," she funds initiatives with defensible economics.
- **Overpromising Tech Vendors:** Claire has been burned by vaporware and half-implemented solutions. She now demands proof, not pilots.
- **Unclear Accountability:** She distrusts initiatives that lack a direct owner, clear performance benchmarks, or governance models.
- **Opaque Algorithms:** If an AI agent cannot explain its decision, it is a liability. Claire won't sign off on anything that compromises auditability or opens the firm to reputational risk.
- **Tech Budget Creep:** She sees AI platforms eating into CapEx and OpEx without yielding proportional benefit. She wants a clear line of sight from investment to impact.

Mental Models

- **Everything Is a Cost Center or a Profit Lever:** If you cannot quantify how the agent moves the needle, it does not matter.

- **First-Order Impact Over Future Promise:** She won't greenlight "potential." She funds what delivers this year and may scale next year.
- **Finance Is the Client:** If you cannot sell the initiative to Finance, you haven't made the case.
- **Simplicity Scales:** Agents that reduce complexity, not add to it, will always get her attention.
- **Trust Is Auditable:** If the agent's decision logic cannot be explained, she assumes it will be rejected by auditors, regulators, or the board.

Five Most Significant Principles to Claire

1. Principle 2: Outcomes Matter – Design for Business Outcomes.
2. Principle 16: Fix First, Then Automate – Do Not Automate a Broken Process.
3. Principle 18: Reveal Hidden ROI_2 – Use Agent Data to Surface Latent Problems and Drive Actionable Insights.
4. Principle 19: Prove the Return – Every Agent Needs an Economic Justification.
5. Principle 20: Govern the Future – The Human:Agent Ratio Is Not Just a Number; It Is a Corporate Truth Serum.

Key Messages for Claire

AI agents are financial levers, not experiments. The book shows how to turn agent deployment into measurable ROI and cost efficiency.

Every agent must justify its economics. "Prove the Return" speaks directly to her gatekeeping role in capital allocation.

Agents can uncover hidden profit pools. By surfacing inefficiencies and latent value, agents expand enterprise margin in ways finance can measure and report.

Governance is financial discipline. The Human:Agent ratio gives her a continuous metric to evaluate productivity, scale, and workforce balance.

CFO sponsorship safeguards shareholder credibility. Claire ensures AI initiatives are not only funded but also defensible in analyst calls, investor briefings, and boardrooms.

Personalized Chapter Excerpts

Chapter 1 – Strategic Deployment and Execution

For Claire, outcomes, not intentions, determine capital allocation. Principles such as "Outcomes Matter" help ensure that every AI agent proposal is tied to hard performance metrics, rather than abstract innovation language. This allows her to defend funding decisions to the board and investors with confidence.

Chapter 3 – Economic Justification and Return on Investment

A CFO's lens is disciplined: no project survives without a clear ROI story. Principles like "Fix First, Then Automate" and "Reveal Hidden ROI_2" equip Claire with frameworks to cut through innovation theater, spotlight cost savings, and monetize efficiencies that otherwise remain invisible.

"Prove the Return" resonates strongly with finance leaders. For Claire, this means not only approving capital but also integrating ROI checkpoints into operating scorecards to prevent AI programs from drifting into uncontrolled spending.

Measurement is Claire's safeguard. The Human:Agent ratio provides her with a quantifiable governance lever that links transformation spending to productivity improvements and reduces ambiguity when reporting to stakeholders.

Executive Persona – Chief Technology Officer

Name: Rafael Montes

Age: 44

Title: Chief Technology Officer

Company: Global 300 Multinational Conglomerate (Financial Services + Logistics + Infrastructure)

Location: London, UK

Education: MSc in Systems Engineering, Imperial College London; BEng in Computer Science, Universidad Politécnica de Madrid

Background: 20+ years in enterprise IT, digital transformation, and platform modernization roles across three continents. Former CIO, now CTO with global oversight

Aspiration: To modernize infrastructure, reduce technical debt, and scale AI agents as enterprise-grade middleware

Fears: Fragmented deployments, vendor lock-in, and AI projects that increase complexity without delivering durable value

Challenges

- Business-led agent deployments are lacking architectural discipline
- Pressure to modernize legacy systems while maintaining uptime and compliance
- Vendor sprawl and lack of interoperability
- AI projects that bypass platform governance
- Technical debt disguised as innovation

Rafael needs more than demos; he needs scalable architecture, observability, and integration discipline.

Strategic Profile

Rafael is a scale-focused CTO who treats agents as infrastructure. He embeds AI into enterprise architecture to modernize systems, reduce latency, and ensure resilience. His mission: deploy agents that are modular, observable, and built to last – without adding technical debt or compromising platform integrity.

Motivations

- **Modernize the Stack:** Accelerate platform transformation without introducing new technical debt.
- **Reduce Latency, Increase Intelligence:** Optimize decision speed and event-handling time.
- **Control Vendor Sprawl:** Favor modular, reusable AI assets over bespoke, vendor-locked deployments.
- **Establish Standards:** Build a globally compliant, cloud-native agent architecture framework.
- **Preserve Talent Leverage:** Focus senior engineers on scalable patterns, not brittle integrations.

Frustrations

- **Fragmented Agent Deployments:** Rogue code at scale from isolated business-led projects.
- **Shadow IT and Vendor Overreach:** Third-party deployments misaligned with enterprise architecture.
- **Overengineered Models:** Agents requiring exotic hardware or constant retraining don't scale.
- **Lack of Platform Thinking:** One-off AI projects that ignore reuse, observability, and security.
- **Tech Debt Camouflage:** AI wins by masking broken processes or integrations.

Mental Models

- **Architect First, Experiment Later:** No "fail fast" in production – patterns over proofs.
- **Observability Is Non-Negotiable:** Agents must be auditable, measurable, and telemetry-integrated.
- **Minimal Viable Interface:** Simplicity drives usage – avoid overwhelming users.
- **Durable Design:** Must last 18–24 months in production without major upkeep.
- **Do Not Automate Broken Things:** Fix the process before automating it.

Five Most Significant Principles to Rafael

1. Principle 12: Make It Mission Infrastructure – Treat Your AI Agent Ecosystem Like Critical Infrastructure, Not a Side Project.
2. Principle 14: Invisible Integration – Design Agents That Blend Seamlessly Into Existing Workflows.
3. Principle 16: Fix First, Then Automate – Do Not Automate a Broken Process.
4. Principle 34: Design for Drift – Build Agents That Adapt as the Business Evolves.
5. Principle 35: Outcome Over Output – Let Agents Speak Through Outcomes, Not Explanations.

Key Messages for Rafael

- Infrastructure first. Agents must be engineered into the enterprise stack as mission-critical systems.
- Fix before scaling. Automating broken processes increases fragility and tech debt.
- Integration drives adoption. Seamless embedding into workflows is key to scale.
- Adaptability is resilience. Agents must evolve with business shifts.
- Impact is more influential than code. Outcomes build trust and drive enterprise value.

Personalized Chapter Excerpts

Chapter 2 – Design Principles and Engineering Discipline

"Make It Mission Infrastructure" affirms Rafael's belief that agents must be built into the enterprise backbone with the same rigor as payment rails, risk engines, and data platforms. "Invisible Integration" supports his view that adoption occurs only when agents seamlessly integrate into workflows.

Chapter 3 – Economic Justification and Return on Investment

"Fix First, Then Automate" resonates with Rafael's frustration at automating broken workflows. He uses this principle to push for process re-engineering before coding begins.

Chapter 5 – Innovation, Ecosystem, and Adaptability

"Design for Drift" reflects Rafael's view that business and technology are in constant flux. Agents must adapt to evolving models, regulations, and expectations.

Chapter 6 – Trust, Transparency, and Selectivity

"Outcomes Over Output" helps Rafael shift conversations from technical jargon to business impact. In boardrooms, outcomes win influence.

Executive Persona – Chief Human Resources Officer

Name: Simone Laurent
Age: 53
Title: Chief Human Resources Officer
Company: Global 300 Professional Services & Technology Firm
Location: Paris, France (Global HQ), oversees workforce in 38 countries
Education: MSc in Organizational Psychology, HEC Paris; BA in International Labor Relations, Sciences Po
Background: 20+ years in HR, talent transformation, and leadership development across technology, consulting, and financial services sectors
Aspiration: To prepare the workforce for an AI-powered future that enhances trust, belonging, and human capability
Fears: Disengagement, cultural resistance, and agents that feel like surveillance rather than support

Challenges

- Tech deployments that ignore human impact
- Lack of a communication strategy around agent rollouts
- Overemphasis on efficiency over empowerment
- Insufficient frontline involvement in agent design
- No upskilling tied to agent deployment

Simone needs more than automation strategies; she needs human-centered design, emotional intelligence, and cultural buy-in.

Strategic Profile

Simone is a people-first transformation leader. She designs future-fit talent ecosystems and ensures AI adoption enhances trust, belonging, and capability. Her mission: embed agents that empower, not replace, humans while preserving psychological safety and cultural integrity across a global workforce.

Motivations

- **Human–AI Collaboration:** Agents should augment talent, not erode trust.
- **Skills Relevance:** Close the digital fluency gap through real-time learning.
- **Experience at Scale:** Use agents to streamline onboarding and feedback.
- **Cultural Buy-In:** Emotion drives adoption, especially among managers.
- **Change Without Fear:** Position agents as empowering through design and narrative.

Frustrations

- **Tech That Ignores People:** Solves technical problems but creates morale issues.
- **Lack of Communication Strategy:** No emotional framing leads to resistance.
- **Overemphasis on Efficiency:** FTE reduction as the only metric is reductive.
- **Insufficient Frontline Involvement:** Agents must be co-designed with users.
- **No Upskilling Tied to Deployment:** Learning must accompany rollout.

Mental Models

- **What You Announce, You Activate:** Messaging shapes mindset.
- **Adoption = Identity:** Tools must reinforce employee value.
- **Fear Blocks Fluency:** Agents must feel like coworkers, not surveillance.
- **Co-Creation Builds Trust:** Involvement reduces resistance.
- **Empowerment Is the Ultimate KPI:** Competence drives scale.

Five Most Significant Principles to Simone

1. Principle 9: Create Craveable Agents – Build Agents That Others Want to Use.
2. Principle 15: Zero-Learning Curve – Design Agents That Just Work. No Training Required.
3. Principle 22: Agents Lift Leaders – Agents Make Leaders Look Good.
4. Principle 28: Win the Frontline – Build Emotional Buy-In With Frontline Teams.
5. Principle 29: Recode the Org DNA – Reinvent the Operating Model Around Agents.

Key Messages for Simone

- Agents are part of the employee experience. Design must be intuitive and craveable.
- Agents should elevate, not replace, leaders. Protect leadership credibility.
- The frontline is emotional territory. Trust and empowerment drive adoption.
- AI demands a rewiring of talent systems. Reinvent roles and org design.
- Culture is the real transformation engine. Simone is the steward of workforce confidence.

Personalized Chapter Excerpts

Chapter 2 – Design Principles and Engineering Discipline

"Create Craveable Agents" reinforces Simone's belief that the best tools feel like consumer products employees want to use. "Zero-Learning Curve" ensures agents work intuitively, lowering anxiety and protecting morale.

Chapter 4 – Leadership, Influence, and Political Buy-In

"Agents Lift Leaders" is a key part of Simone's strategy. Agents should extend – not replace – leadership influence. Empowered managers accelerate adoption.

"Win the Frontline" gives Simone the playbook to build emotional buy-in. She knows cultural adoption is emotional first, rational second.

Chapter 5 – Innovation, Ecosystem, and Adaptability

"Recode the Org DNA" validates Simone's agenda to redesign roles, career paths, and performance systems around agents.

Executive Persona – Chief Marketing Officer

Name: Mo Nasser

Age: 41

Title: Chief Marketing Officer

Company: Global 300 Consumer & Financial Services Enterprise

Location: New York, NY (Global HQ), oversees marketing in 42 countries

Education: MBA in Marketing & Strategy, Wharton; BA in Economics, University of California, Berkeley

Background: 15+ years in brand strategy, customer experience, and digital transformation. Led marketing at two Fortune 100 firms before current role. Known for pioneering data-driven personalization and orchestrating global rebrands

Aspiration: To make marketing a measurable growth engine powered by AI-driven personalization and creative scale

Fears: Losing brand relevance in a world of instant, contextual, and seamless customer expectations

Challenges

- Fragmented data systems blocking unified personalization
- Pressure to prove marketing's revenue contribution
- Slow campaign cycles compared to digital-native competitors
- Tension with sales over marketing's impact on growth
- Compliance bottlenecks slowing speed-to-market

Mo needs more than creative ideas; he needs agent-powered systems that deliver speed, personalization, and measurable growth.

Strategic Profile

Mo is a growth-focused marketing leader. He uses AI agents to personalize customer journeys, accelerate creative output, and prove marketing's revenue impact. His mission: transform marketing into a real-time engine of relevance, speed, and measurable business outcomes.

Motivations

- **Personalization at Scale:** Deliver tailored customer interactions across channels, in real time.
- **Speed to Market:** Accelerate content production, campaign testing, and product launches.
- **Revenue Accountability:** Tie marketing initiatives directly to pipeline, conversion, and lifetime value.
- **Creative Amplification:** Free human teams to focus on big ideas while agents handle production.
- **Data-Driven Storytelling:** Unify fragmented data into narratives that drive trust and loyalty.

Frustrations

- **Siloed Data:** Fragmented systems block unified personalization.
- **Vanity Metrics:** KPIs like impressions or clicks don't prove financial impact.
- **Slow Campaign Cycles:** Manual processes slow down competitive response.
- **Resistance From Sales:** Sales leaders question marketing's contribution to growth.
- **Compliance Bottlenecks:** Reviews delay launches, especially in regulated markets.

Mental Models

- **"Marketing must show me the money."** A brand without revenue proof is indulgence.
- **"Personalization is power."** Consumers trust brands that feel relevant in the moment.
- **"Creative speed equals market share."** Fast brands win visibility and loyalty.
- **"AI is the new media team."** Agents are the backbone of next-gen marketing.
- **"Data is the story."** Metrics are the narrative that investors and customers believe.

Five Most Significant Principles to Mo

1. Principle 2: Outcomes Matter – Design for Business Outcomes.
2. Principle 11: Choreograph the Unmissable Moment – Showcase an Emotionally Resonant Win.

3. Principle 18: Reveal Hidden ROI_2 – Use Agent Data to Surface Latent Problems and Drive Actionable Insights.
4. Principle 26: Stage the Win – Use Agent Wins to Create Executive Theater.
5. Principle 29: Recode the Org DNA – Reinvent the Operating Model Around Agents.

Key Messages for Mo

- Agents are storytelling platforms. The first deployment must be a showpiece.
- Marketing must prove outcomes. Tie agents to revenue and customer impact.
- Data becomes narrative. Use agent insights to tell board-ready stories.
- Wins must be staged. Pilots are theater to persuade and scale.
- Marketing's DNA must evolve. Agents enable speed, personalization, and measurable growth.

Personalized Chapter Excerpts

Chapter 2 – Design Principles and Engineering Discipline

"Choreograph the Unmissable Moment" resonates deeply with Mo. The first agent deployment should be dramatic and strategically staged to prove what's possible and position marketing as the hub of transformation.

Chapter 3 – Economic Justification and Return on Investment

Mo demands revenue impact, not vanity metrics. "Reveal Hidden ROI_2" reinforce his belief that agents must prove growth contribution and retention.

Chapter 4 – Leadership, Influence, and Political Buy-In

"Stage the Win" is central to Mo's playbook. Every successful pilot is theater – an opportunity to script impact, secure C-suite attention, and amplify adoption.

Chapter 5 – Innovation, Ecosystem, and Adaptability

"Recode the Org DNA" gives Mo the rationale to rebuild workflows and customer experience delivery around agents. It's a license to modernize marketing's operating system.

Appendix B

Measure Performance

OKRs

Objectives and key results (OKRs) are among the most effective tools for aligning strategy with execution. The value of OKRs begins with alignment. In large organizations, strategy can become diluted as it moves down the hierarchy. OKRs establish a direct connection between the boardroom's intent and frontline actions, preventing drift, reducing confusion, and ensuring teams at every level understand not just what to deliver but why it matters. In the context of AI agents, OKRs are critical for demonstrating legitimacy. By setting objectives connected to business goals, such as improving the Human:Agent ratio, reducing time-to-decision, or generating new revenue streams, organizations demonstrate that agents are not just novelties but also strategic assets. OKRs thus provide economic and political justification for ongoing investment.

They foster transparency, enabling leadership to objectively track progress and credibly communicate success stories to stakeholders, regulators, and investors. OKRs are essential because they operationalize ambition, enforce accountability, and demonstrate legitimacy. They are the mechanism through which vision becomes action. In the playbook of enterprise transformation, OKRs act as the bridge between intent and impact. Here are the most essential OKRs. They are designed with a balance of strategic intent (objective) and measurable outcomes (key results).

Chapter 1 – Strategic Deployment and Execution

Principle: Strategy before theater. Deploy with discipline, not hype.

Objective 1: Ensure all agent deployments align directly with enterprise business objectives.

- KR1: 100% of deployed agents have documented business outcome linkages.
- KR2: Achieve $\geq$15% measurable business impact (cost reduction, revenue growth, risk reduction) within 6 months of deployment.
- KR3: Reduce innovation-only initiatives with no economic justification to <5% of the total pipeline.

Objective 2: Deploy AI agents with disciplined sequencing and governance.

- KR1: Establish deployment sequencing roadmap with ≥90% adherence rate.
- KR2: Reduce deployment cycle time by 30% without increasing defect rates.
- KR3: Ensure 95% of stakeholders rate deployment readiness as "high" before launch.

Objective 3: Scale agents responsibly while avoiding organizational chaos.

- KR1: Cap incremental deployments at <20% workforce exposure per phase.
- KR2: Maintain <2% disruption rate in business workflows during scaling.
- KR3: Ensure 100% of scaled deployments are supported by governance playbooks.

Chapter 2 – Design Principles and Engineering Discipline

Principle: Form follows function. Build agents people want to use and trust.
Objective 1: Engineer agents that maximize adoption through usability and trust.

- KR1: 85%+ user satisfaction scores within 3 months of rollout.
- KR2: Achieve <5% user-reported friction incidents per quarter.
- KR3: Reach ≥70% repeat usage rate within 60 days of launch.

Objective 2: Position the first agent as a showcase for organizational credibility.

- KR1: Launch at least one showpiece agent generating measurable PR/leadership impact.
- KR2: Secure ≥3 executive endorsements citing the agent as value-creating.
- KR3: Achieve 90% awareness of the flagship agent within the intended business unit.

Objective 3: Institutionalize design and engineering discipline.

- KR1: 100% of new agents are designed with the zero-training-curve principle applied.
- KR2: Embed trust-by-design guidelines into 100% of engineering sprints.
- KR3: Integrate agents into ≥80% of targeted workflows without user disruption.

Chapter 3 – Economic Justification and Return on Investment

Principle: No economics, no adoption. Agents must prove financial worth.
Objective 1: Guarantee economic validation of every AI agent.

- KR1: 100% of deployed agents have an ROI analysis conducted pre-launch.

- KR2: Eliminate agents without a clear economic justification by Q4.
- KR3: Achieve average ROI ≥ 2.5x within 12 months of deployment.

Objective 2: Optimize process integrity before automation.

- KR1: Ensure 90% of targeted processes are audited and optimized pre-automation.
- KR2: Reduce rework/failure rates by 40% in automated workflows.
- KR3: Deliver ≥10% cost savings per process automated.

Objective 3: Drive measurable Human:Agent ratio improvements.

- KR1: Improve baseline Human:Agent ratio by at least 15% YoY.
- KR2: Publish a quarterly dashboard showing ratio and impact metrics.
- KR3: Benchmark ratio vs. top-3 competitors and achieve leadership position within 2 years.

Chapter 4 – Leadership, Influence, and Political Buy-In

Principle: Adoption is political. Agents succeed when leaders and power centers align.
Objective 1: Secure leadership endorsement and alignment.

- KR1: ≥90% of executives confirm agents align with the strategic agenda.
- KR2: Gain ≥3 public executive endorsements per major agent launch.
- KR3: Achieve 100% leader participation in quarterly agent review forums.

Objective 2: Build stakeholder maps and influence coalitions.

- KR1: Create power maps for 100% of major agent deployments.
- KR2: Engage at least 80% of identified gatekeepers pre-deployment.
- KR3: Convert ≥70% of functional leaders into active sponsors within 6 months.

Objective 3: Drive frontline adoption through emotional and practical buy-in.

- KR1: Reach ≥75% frontline adoption rate within 90 days of deployment.
- KR2: Reduce frontline resistance incidents by 50% vs. previous rollouts.
- KR3: Deliver at least two "staged wins" per deployment for cultural reinforcement.

Chapter 5 – Innovation, Ecosystem, and Adaptability

Principle: Agents are not projects; they are ecosystems designed for adaptability.
Objective 1: Embed agents into the organizational DNA.

- KR1: Redesign ≥2 operating model functions to be agent-first per year.
- KR2: Retire ≥10% legacy processes annually in favor of agent-driven models.
- KR3: Introduce ≥3 net-new roles to support agent ecosystems by year-end.

Objective 2: Create adaptive, learning-driven agent ecosystems.

- KR1: Ensure 100% of agents have built-in learning loop mechanisms.
- KR2: Achieve 80%+ accuracy improvement in agent performance after 6 months.
- KR3: Respond to ≥90% of real-time business triggers within 5 seconds.

Objective 3: Scale innovations based on pain-point resolution.

- KR1: Identify and prioritize the op-10 enterprise pain points annually for agent design.
- KR2: Scale ≥70% of agents that deliver validated cures for identified pains.
- KR3: Achieve ≥20% YoY revenue/cost benefit from scalable cures.

Chapter 6 – Trust, Transparency, and Selectivity

Principle: Trust is earned through restraint, not disclosure. Agents must inspire confidence.
Objective 1: Strengthen user trust through selective transparency.

- KR1: Publish agent limitations in ≥90% of internal communications.
- KR2: Ensure 95% of the user base confirms confidence in agent accuracy.
- KR3: Reduce trust-related escalations by 60% YoY.

Objective 2: Build accountability into agent governance.

- KR1: 100% of surfaced "uncomfortable truths" accompanied by an action plan.
- KR2: Ensure agent audit reports are completed for ≥95% of deployments.
- KR3: Establish clear stewardship owners for 100% of agent categories.

Objective 3: Demonstrate value through outcomes, not outputs.

- KR1: Tie 90% of agent dashboards to business KPIs instead of technical metrics.
- KR2: Reduce reporting noise (non-KPI output metrics) by 50%.
- KR3: Ensure ≥3 case studies per year showing outcome-driven success.

Chapter 7 – Adoption, Scale, and User-Centricity

Principle: Scale is earned, not announced. User validation creates momentum.
Objective 1: Prove adoption through strategic pilots.

- KR1: Run ≥5 pilots per year with measurable business outcomes.
- KR2: Convert ≥70% of pilots into scaled deployments within 12 months.
- KR3: Reduce skepticism scores among stakeholders by 40% post-pilot.

Objective 2: Scale incrementally based on validated success.

- KR1: Increase user adoption rate by ≥20% per scaled release.
- KR2: Expand to 3+ additional business units annually post-pilot success.
- KR3: Keep deployment rollback rate <3% across all scaling phases.

Objective 3: Leverage acquisitions and partnerships to accelerate adoption.

- KR1: Execute ≥2 strategic acquisitions/partnerships per year for agent capabilities.
- KR2: Achieve ≥15% acceleration in adoption timelines through acquired solutions.
- KR3: Integrate 100% of acquired capabilities into the agent ecosystem within 9 months.

Appendix C

Learning and Development Objectives

Learning & development (L&D) objectives are essential for building organizational capability. They define the knowledge, skills, and behaviors needed to execute strategy and ensure that leadership programs and workforce training align with critical capabilities. In the context of AI adoption, learning objectives focus on building trust in technology, understanding economic models, and achieving political alignment. These skills are vital for successful, large-scale implementation.

Clear objectives democratize strategy by enabling individuals at all levels to contribute meaningfully. When people understand what they need to learn and why, they become active participants in change. Learning objectives also provide a framework for measurement, much like OKRs, helping assess whether leaders can secure buy-in, engineers can build trustworthy systems, and employees can integrate AI into workflows.

They also mitigate risks, addressing cultural resistance, skills gaps, and ethical concerns by preparing individuals through targeted learning in trust, accountability, and adaptive design. Codified and reinforced, these objectives reshape behavior and support AI as an adaptive change process. Ultimately, they align capabilities with ambition, reduce risk, and turn vision into action.

Chapter 1 – Strategic Deployment and Execution

Principle: Strategy before theater. Deploy with discipline, not hype.
L&D Objectives:

1. Equip leaders and practitioners with the ability to translate enterprise strategy into actionable AI agent deployment roadmaps that are sequenced, disciplined, and outcome-driven.
2. Develop organizational literacy on execution governance, guiding teams to deploy incrementally, measure readiness, and prevent hype-driven rollouts that damage credibility.

Chapter 2 – Design Principles and Engineering Discipline

Principle: Form follows function. Build agents people want to use and trust.
L&D Objectives:

1. Train engineering and product teams to design agents that are naturally intuitive, trust-focused, and smoothly integrated into workflows without needing end-user training.
2. Build organizational capability to treat agents as mission-critical infrastructure, teaching leaders to balance showpiece innovation with scalable, resilient systems thinking.

Chapter 3 – Economic Justification and Return on Investment

Principle: No economics, no adoption. Agents must prove financial worth.
L&D Objectives:

1. Enable executives and managers to perform ROI-driven assessments of AI agents, ensuring economic justification is embedded from concept to deployment.
2. Train operations and finance teams to leverage agent data for surfacing hidden value, measuring Human:Agent ratios, and aligning automation with cost and productivity outcomes.

Chapter 4 – Leadership, Influence, and Political Buy-In

Principle: Adoption is political. Agents succeed when leaders and power centers align.
L&D Objectives:

1. Develop leadership fluency in mapping organizational power structures and using agent deployments to reinforce, not threaten, existing authority lines.
2. Train change leaders to build narratives, stage symbolic wins, and secure both executive sponsors and frontline emotional buy-in to accelerate adoption.

Chapter 5 – Innovation, Ecosystem, and Adaptability

Principle: Agents are not projects; they are ecosystems designed for adaptability.
L&D Objectives:

1. Teach leaders and technologists to design agents as part of adaptive ecosystems, embedding live learning loops, real-time response, and long-term scalability.

2. Build organizational capability to spot high-value pain points, scale cures, and recode operating models around agent-first structures rather than legacy processes.

Chapter 6 – Trust, Transparency, and Selectivity

Principle: Trust is earned through restraint, not disclosure. Agents must inspire confidence.
L&D Objectives:

1. Train executives and employees to communicate agent outputs with restraint, selectively revealing outcomes to build long-term trust instead of overwhelming stakeholders with noise.
2. Build organizational confidence by teaching teams to expose agent limitations responsibly, pair insights with accountability, and use transparency to boost credibility.

Chapter 7 – Adoption, Scale, and User-Centricity

Principle: Scale is earned, not announced. User validation creates momentum.
L&D Objectives:

1. Equip leaders with the skills to use pilot programs as persuasion tools, converting small wins into cultural momentum and political capital for scaled deployment.
2. Develop organizational fluency in scaling strategies, teaching teams to expand adoption incrementally, leveraging acquisitions, and ensuring user validation drives momentum.

Executive L&D Curriculum: Scaling AI Agents With Power and Precision

Designed for an executive offsite, each chapter becomes a module, with objectives, formats, and time allocations, as depicted in Figure C.1. The structure is meant to be practical, experiential, and directly tied to enterprise execution. The offsite creates a progression from **Strategy** → **Design** → **Economics** → **Influence** → **Ecosystem** → **Trust** → **Adoption**.

Executive L&D Curriculum: Scaling AI Agents With Power and Precision				
Program Overview • Target Audience: C-Suite, EVPs, functional leaders, transformation executives • Format: 2–3-day intensive, modular design (can be condensed into half-day boardroom workshops or extended into multi-week executive education) • Approach: Case-based learning, experiential simulations, peer-to-peer debates, and applied design sprints				
	Session	*Learning Objective*	*Agenda*	*Deliverable*
Day 1	Module 1: Strategic Deployment and Execution (2 hours 30 min)	Deploy agents with discipline, sequencing, and measurable outcomes.	• Case Study Workshop (90 mins): Analyze a failed hype-driven AI deployment vs. a disciplined, outcome-driven rollout. • Simulation (60 mins): Executive role-play deciding whether to launch an "AI showcase" under market pressure vs. waiting for readiness.	• Each participant creates a 90-day deployment roadmap tied to business goals.
Day 1	Module 2: Design Principles and Engineering Discipline (2 hours 45 min)	Build agents people trust, use, and rely on.	• Hands-On Lab (120 mins): Redesign a poorly adopted chatbot into a craveable, zero-training agent. • Executive Dialogue (45 mins): Debate "Spectacle vs. Infrastructure," when to launch a flashy showpiece vs. when to harden the ecosystem.	• A checklist of agent design principles tailored for the participant's enterprise.
Day 1	Module 3: Economic Justification and Return on Investment (2 hours 30 min)	Ground every agent in financial value.	• Finance Sprint (90 mins): Teams calculate ROI, cost savings, and Human-Agent ratio for a sample business process. • Dashboard Workshop (60 mins): Build an agent performance scorecard that surfaces hidden ROI.	• Draft ROI framework to take back to their enterprise CFO.

Figure C.1 Three-day executive L&D curriculum: Scaling AI agents with power and precision. Diagram by BMO Financial Group.

Day 2	Module 4: Leadership, Influence, and Political Buy-In (2 hours 15 min)	Secure leadership sponsorship and political alignment.	• Stakeholder Mapping Exercise (75 mins): Create power maps for a fictional enterprise, then role-play lobbying key leaders. • Executive Theater Simulation (60 mins): Stage an "Agent Win" for the board, practice positioning outcomes as leadership capital.	• Stakeholder map and staged-win plan for a priority use case.
Day 2	Module 5: Innovation, Ecosystem, and Adaptability (2 hours 45 min)	Treat agents as adaptive ecosystems, not projects.	• Ecosystem Mapping Workshop (90 mins): Redesign an operating model around agents, replacing legacy roles with net-new agent-enabled roles. • Learning Loop Lab (75 mins): Participants design a feedback loop where agents learn in real time from user behavior.	• A draft "Agent Ecosystem Blueprint" for one business unit.
	Module 6: Trust, Transparency, and Selectivity (2 hours 30 min)	Earn trust through restraint, accountability, and selective disclosure.	• Crisis Simulation (90 mins): Manage an agent failure scenario, decide how much to disclose, to whom, and when. • Trust Framework Workshop (60 mins): Design a trust-by-design playbook for agent governance.	• Trust and accountability framework customized to their organization.

Figure C.1 (Continued)

Day 3	Module 7: Adoption, Scale, and User-Centricity (2 hours 30 min)	Drive adoption through pilots, persuasion, and user validation.	• Pilot-to-Scale Sprint (90 mins): Teams design a pilot plan, define KPIs, and simulate presenting results to skeptical executives. • Procurement & Partnership Debate (60 mins): When to build vs. acquire to accelerate adoption.	• Adoption playbook with a pilot strategy, scaling sequence, and acquisition filter.
	Program Capstone: The Boardroom Simulation (3 hours)	N/A	• Scenario: Each executive team presents a comprehensive AI agent strategy (deployment, design, economics, leadership buy-in, ecosystem, trust, adoption). • Format: Board-style pitch to a panel of peers who act as the "Chair, CFO, CHRO, Regulator, and Activist Investor." • Outcome: Stress-test the strategy under real-world political, economic, and regulatory pressures.	• N/A

Figure C.1 (Continued)

About the Author

Dr. Kristin Milchanowski is Chief Artificial Intelligence and Data Officer for BMO Financial Group and is a member of BMO's Technology and Operations Executive Committee. Kristin is responsible for driving BMO's AI, data, analytics, and quantum strategies, championing a transformative AI roadmap to accelerate BMO's Digital First, AI-Empowered strategy.

Kristin is a global executive and board member with over 20 years of experience, specializing in AI, decision sciences, and quantum computing. Kristin is an associate fellow of the University of Oxford Saïd Business School, where she completed post-graduate studies in AI; a lifelong learner, she holds a PhD in decision sciences, a Master of Business Administration, a Master of Theology, and a Bachelor of Business Administration.

Formerly, Kristin held the following positions: Global Innovation Partner/Principal at EY, Chief Data Scientist at Morgan Stanley, and Head of Global Financial Crimes Compliance Technology and Model Management at JPMorgan. Kristin served on the foundation board of Children's National Hospital in Washington, D.C. She is a licensed race car driver and was formerly an advisory board member of Automobili Lamborghini. Kristin wrote and illustrated a children's book, *Tell Me Henry*, to advocate for more diversity in children's literature.

For media inquiries, see: http://www.bmo.com/innovationhub/contactus

Index

For Product Safety Concerns and Information please contact our EU representative GPSR@taylorandfrancis.com Taylor & Francis Verlag GmbH, Kaufingerstraße 24, 80331 München, Germany